SAP ABAP Objects Interview Questions: SAP ABAP Objects Frequently Asked Questions

Compiled By Terry Sanchez-Clark
Edited by Jim Stewart

ABAP Objects Interview Questions**Error! Bookmark not defined.**: ABAP Objects Frequently Asked Questions

ISBN: 978-1-06332-022-1

Edited by: Jamie Fisher

The programs in this book have been included for instructional value only.

The publisher does not offer any warranties or representations and does not accept any liabilities with respect to the programs.

Printed in the United States of America

Please visit our website at www.sapcookbook.com

Table of Contents

Question 45: Controlling objects 62

Question 67: Problem with local class, static private attribute, and public method 91

Introduction

What Is ABAP Objects?

ABAP Objects is a new concept in R/3 Release 4.0. The term has two meanings. On the one hand, it stands for the entire ABAP runtime environment. On the other hand, it represents the object-oriented extension of the ABAP language.

The Runtime Environment

The new name ABAP Objects for the entire ABAP runtime environment is an indication of the way in which SAP has, for some time, been moving towards object orientation, and of its commitment to pursuing this line further. The ABAP Workbench allows you to create R/3 Repository objects such as programs, authorization objects, lock objects, Customizing objects, and so on. Using function modules, you can encapsulate functions in separate programs with a defined interface. The Business Object Repository (BOR) allows you to create SAP Business Objects for internal and external use (DCOM/CORBA). Until now, object-oriented techniques have been used exclusively in system design, and have not been supported by the ABAP language.

The Object-Oriented Language Extension

ABAP Objects is a complete set of object-oriented statements that has been introduced into the ABAP language. This object-oriented extension of ABAP builds on the existing language, and is fully compatible with it. You can use ABAP Objects in existing programs, and can also use "conventional" ABAP in new ABAP Objects programs.

ABAP Objects supports object-oriented programming. Object orientation (OO), also know as the object-oriented paradigm, is a programming model that unites data and functions in objects. The rest of the ABAP language is primarily intended for structured programming, where data is stored in a structured form in database tables and function-oriented programs access and work with it.

The object-oriented enhancement of ABAP is based on the models of Java and C++. It is compatible with external object interfaces such as DCOM and CORBA. The implementation of object-oriented elements in the kernel of the ABAP language has considerably increased response times when you work with ABAP Objects. SAP Business Objects and GUI objects - already object-oriented themselves - will also profit from being incorporated in ABAP Objects.

ABAP Objects

Object orientation in ABAP is an extension of the ABAP language that makes available the advantages of object-oriented programming, such as encapsulation, interfaces, and inheritance. This helps to simplify applications and make them more controllable.

ABAP Objects is fully compatible with the existing language, so you can use existing statements and modularization units in programs that use ABAP Objects, and can also use ABAP Objects in existing ABAP programs.

ALV

Questions and Answers

Question 1: ALV Control - Field Catalog Dump

I have a local structure 'st_duty' (prepared from 2 tables) and an internal table 'it_duty'.

When I am preparing the 'Field' catalog for this, it is giving a dump.

The code given is as follows:

```
DATA: it_fcat1 TYPE TABLE OF lvc_s_fcat,
wa_fcat1 TYPE lvc_s_fcat.

clear wa_fcat1.
wa_fcat1-coltext = 'Duty code'.
wa_fcat1-REF_FIELD = 'DUTCODE'.
wa_fcat1-REF_TABLE = '/OBIZ/ZMB_BEDUT'.
wa_fcat1-FIELDNAME = 'DUTCODE'.
wa_fcat1-col_pos = 1.
MODIFY it_fcat1 FROM wa_fcat1.

clear wa_fcat1. "At this Point it is giving short
dump"
wa_fcat1-coltext = 'Description'.
wa_fcat1-REF_FIELD = 'CODDESC'.
wa_fcat1-REF_TABLE = '/OBIZ/ZCM_CODMAS'.
wa_fcat1-FIELDNAME = 'CODDESC'.
wa_fcat1-col_pos = 2.
MODIFY it_fcat1 FROM wa_fcat1.

Short Dump Message as given below:

Error analysis:
You attempted to change, delete or create a line in
the internal table
"\PROGRAM=SAPMZ_BOE_DETAILS_OBIZ\DATA=IT_FCAT1", but
no valid
cursor exists for the table.
```

Possible reasons:

1. The relevent ABAP/4 statement does not include the addition "...INDEX...", although the statement is not
inside a "LOOP...ENDLOOP" loop processing this table.

2. The relevent ABAP/4 statement was called from within a "LOOP...ENDLOOP" loop after a DELETE "\PROGRAM=SAPMZ_BOE_DETAILS_OBIZ\DATA=IT_FCAT1".

What can be the reason for this?

A: You can try the following to modify the field catalog:

Use APPEND Field catalog.

Append “wa_fcat” into “it_fcat”.

When looping through the field catalog, use modify.

Question 2: ALV List generation

I am generating a basic list and from that, I am generating an ALV for detailed list.

```
The problem is when I am coming back to the basic
list and choose a different value, it is always
showing the first value that I selected.
```

What is the solution for this?

A: Check the value coming in the variable at the stament. Just check in the debugging portion.

```
READ LINE SY-CUROW FIELD VALUE WA_ITAB-S_CARRID INTO
T_CARRID
WA_ITAB-S_CONNID INTO T_CONNID.
```

Also try this:

```
clear wa_itab2.
APPEND WA TO WA_ITAB2.


CALL SCREEN 100.
```

After calling the screen, you need to give the “Clear” command.

Question 3: Select rows in ALV grid with

I'm using class "CL_GUI_ALV_GRID" and I want the buttons at the beginning of every row to select it. With the classic function "REUSE_ALV_GRID_DISPLAY", I used the layout parameter box_fieldname:

layout-box_fieldname = 'CBOX'.
Where 'CBOX' is the name field of my internal table in the first position (char1),
and it worked.

With the "CL_GUI_ALV_GRID", there's no parameter 'box_fieldname' but 'BOX_FNAME'.
layout_alv-BOX_FNAME = 'CBOX'.
When I call the method –

```
call method grid->set_table_for_first_display
EXPORTING
is_layout = layout_alv
CHANGING
IT_FIELDCATALOG = it_fieldcat_voci
it_sort = gt_sort_grid[]
it_outtab = gt_voci[].
```

– it doesn't work.
Why did this happen? How can I fix this?

A: It's a little different using the class. First, you need to set the selection module before calling the "SET_TABLE_FOR_FIRST_DISPLAY" method.

Question 4: Getting the sum for each currency in ALV Report

A column has amounts with various currencies.

How can I get the sum quantity for each currency in the ALV Report?

A: Currency value column should have reference to currency code column.

Question 5: Event handling in ALV OOPS with buttons

What is the procedure on handling events in OOPS like interactive reports using events?

A: You can use the event 'HOTSPOT_CLICK' and 'BUTTON_CLICK'. For the sake of simplicity, use the column for the company code as "button" column. Of course you would add an additional column in a real-time report.

Question 6: ALV Regdg

I have to develop a report which has one main heading and that heading is further split into 2/3 more sub headings.

Is it possible to develop this kind of report using ALV?

A sample format is given below:

```
---------------
| Column 1 |
---------------

--------------------------------
| Column 1a | Column 1b |
--------------------------------
```

If it's not possible using ALV, is there any other option?

A: Try using the top of the page event in ALV. You can also check this example code, there are multiple headers displayed.

Question 7: ALV using ABAP Classes and Objects

I am trying to print the values in my internal table using ALV, and using ABAP classes and objects. The title for columns was picked based on the title specified in the data element. I want to set the title of my columns by my own.

How can I achieve this? A sample code will be of help.

A: You have to build an ALV field catalog for this. You can check the online help: http://help.sap.com/saphelp_47x200/helpdata/en/52/5f060de02d11d2b47d006094192fe3/frameset.htm

Question 8: Display Logo on ALV Grid Report

I am displaying data as ALV Grid using "CALL METHOD CL_SALV_TABLE=>FACTORY".
I am having trouble on how to display the logo on top of the page event.

How can I do that?

A: You can use the class 'cl_salv_form_picture' when writing your headers. Implement the following and pay attention to the FORM 'create_header_and_footer'.

Question 9: ALV Header Regdg

I am using Class 'CL_SALV_TABLE' to generate my ALV report. I also want to display a header for this report.

Is there any method which would help me to achieve this functionality?

A: Here are some code snippets to give you an idea of what you can use. You could also refer to demo program 'SALV_TEST_TABLE' which has everything.

```
data: gr_table   type ref to cl_salv_table.

data:
    lr_display type ref to cl_salv_display_settings,
    header type lvc_title.

....

header = 'test header'.

lr_display = gr_table->get_display_settings( ).

lr_display->set_list_header( header ).
```

Question 10: Change the status in ALV

I call an ALV in a subscreen. In the catalog, there are 2 checkbox in edit mode, so the default status GUI is diferent if I call it with no editable fields.

I want to change the default status GUI than the ALV OO sets automatically. There are two (2) kinds of standard status, the read mode and the editable mode with different controls for each. If the ALV detects any editable field in the catalog, it automatically sets the edit mode status GUI. If there's none, then it sets the basic status GUI. I just want to set the basic status GUI when my list have editable fields.

I want to set the status in read mode, is there any way?

A: You can use field catalog edit = 'X'.

You also have to do this logic yourself. Assuming that you have created your ALV grid instance already, and then you have to code in the PBO module where you set your GUI status

Take note that method ‘IS_READY_FOR_INPUT’ has optional parameter for row number and column number. Thus, it appears that you can specifically ask the grid instance whether a certain column (your checkbox column) is editable or not.

Question 11: Delete function

I find the event TOOLBAR in the class 'CL_GUI_ALV_GRID' in the application which stated: "Change, delete or add GUI elements in the toolbar". I want to delete elements, but there's no information about. There's the example report BCALV_GRID_05, but this one just inserted new elements. I want to delete the standard ones like CL_GUI_ALV_GRID=>MC_FC_DETAIL.

How can I do it?

A: I think you may need to use the option of excluding toolbar buttons from the ALV grid (IT_TOOLBAR_EXCLUDING) while using the 'SET_TABLE_FOR_FIRST_DISPLAY'. Here, you can specify what buttons you want to exclude from display on the ALV grid. With the TOOLBAR event, I think you can only disable the buttons from usage though they are still visible on the toolbar.

Question 12: Hold Multiple Selections in ALV Lists with cl_salv_table

I developed an ALV report using the SALV classes

I noticed that it creates the lateral selection bar that makes you choose one or more records in the list. But changing the selections on the sidebar, I see that it doesn't hold the previously chosen record. I tried to choose contiguous records making drag-and-drop on the sidebar, and it works as well.

I tried to choose not-contiguous records keeping pressed the "Ctrl" key, and it works too.
So I think that the client would want to select contiguous and not-contiguous records only by a single mouse click.

Is it possible to do it, keeping selected the clicked rows one-by-one?

A: No, this is not possible. The GUI controls this and was designed to work like Excel, so you know that this functionality doesn't exist in Excel either. You must hold the CTRL to do random selections.

It is not possible to do editable ALV using the new object model. In order to do this, you would have to revert back to the 'CL_GUI_ALV_GRID' class, or the function module 'REUSE_ALV_GRID_DISPLAY'.

Question 13: Sorting some columns in ALV Grid

I want to tell to the method 'set_table_for_first_display' to make one of the columns not sortable. Let's say the column name is "My Icon".

When the User will highlight column "My icon" and then click on sort buttons in the toolbar, no sort will happen on this column.

I was trying to identify a field in 'lvc_s_sort' which would say "do not sort this column". Is there any?

A: Set the following flags in the 'field catalog' entry for your fixed columns:

```
ls_fcat-key = 'X'.
ls_fcat-fix_column = 'X'.
```

However, fixed columns are always at the left side of the ALV list. You cannot fix columns in the middle or on the right side of the ALV list.

You would need to remove the SORT buttons and then create Custom buttons that do the sorting. You would trigger your SORT code in the PAI of the screen containing the ALV grid.

First thing is that you need a local class as your event handler, copy and paste this code. Here, we are using the name 'ALV_GRID' for your ALV object.

Question 14: ALV Tree

I'm using 'CL_GUI_ALV_TREE'. When I build the hierarchy and set the parameters of a node, I also put IS_NODE_LAYOUT-ISFOLDER = 'X'.

In an event, I have the 'node_key' and I want the characteristic of this node, and in particular if this node is a folder or not.

How can I do this? What is the method to get the layout?

A: I think the method TREE_GET_NODE_LAYOUT is useful. In here, you have the node layout info in 'ES_NODE_LAYOUT' when you supply the node key to 'I_NODE_KEY'.
The method TREE_GET_NODE_LAYOUT is called from method GET_OUTTAB_LINE that returns ES_NODE_LAYOUT.

Question 15: ALV in output using Object Oriented Model

I want to display two ALV in my report output. I have two internal tables and I want one ALV for each internal table.

It will be better if the ALV output is in grid format. How can I do this?

A: You have to define two screen areas as containers for each of the 2 ALVs. Then, construct the ALV grid on each of the areas using the CREATE OBJECT statement passing the container references.

Then use the 'SET_TABLE_FOR_FIRST_DISPLAY', using each of the 2 ALV grid references and passing your internal tables.

Question 16: ALV Reports using ABAP Objects

I am trying to print the values in my internal table using ALV, ABAP classes and objects. In here, I am able to get the total successfully. But I need to get subtotals also, like based on the carrid in table 'sflight'. I need the subtotal of the price for every carrid like 'LH' and 'SQ'.

Here is my code:

```
REPORT znav_report.

DATA: alv TYPE REF TO cl_salv_table,
value1 TYPE REF TO cl_salv_aggregations,
value2 TYPE REF TO cl_salv_aggregation.

DATA: BEGIN OF itab_flight OCCURS 0,
carrid LIKE sflight-carrid,
connid LIKE sflight-connid,
fldate LIKE sflight-fldate,
price LIKE sflight-price,
paymentsum LIKE sflight-paymentsum,
currency LIKE sflight-currency,
END OF itab_flight.
SELECT carrid
connid
fldate
price
paymentsum
```

```
currency
FROM sflight INTO TABLE itab_flight
WHERE carrid = 'LH' OR carrid = 'SQ'.

cl_salv_table=>factory( IMPORTING r_salv_table = alv
CHANGING t_table = itab_flight[] ).

CALL METHOD alv->get_aggregations
RECEIVING
value = value1.

CALL METHOD value1->add_aggregation
EXPORTING
columnname = 'PAYMENTSUM'
aggregation = if_salv_c_aggregation=>total
RECEIVING
value = value2.

alv->display( ).
```

How can I get the subtotals for every different carrid?

A: Go through the following:

```
DATA: alv TYPE REF TO cl_salv_table,
value1 TYPE REF TO cl_salv_aggregations.

data: itab_flight type table of sflight.

data: gr_sorts type ref to cl_salv_sorts.
data: gr_agg type ref to cl_salv_aggregations.


start-of-selection.

select * into table itab_flight from sflight.


cl_salv_table=>factory( IMPORTING r_salv_table = alv
CHANGING t_table = itab_flight[] ).

CALL METHOD alv->get_aggregations
RECEIVING
value = value1.

gr_sorts = alv->get_sorts( ).
gr_sorts->add_sort( columnname = 'CARRID' subtotal =
abap_true ).
value1->add_aggregation( 'PAYMENTSUM' ).


alv->display( ).
```

Question 17: Code stuck

My code is stuck – what is the problem?

```
data : begin of itab_flight occurs 0,
carrid type sflight-carrid,
connid type sflight-connid,
fldate type sflight-fldate,
price type sflight-price,
currency type sflight-currency,
planetype type sflight-planetype,
end of itab_flight.
```

Then, when I perform a select query, it stated “select carrid connid fldate price currency plane type into corresponding fields of table itab_flight from sflight”, it gives me a dump.

How can I resolve this?

A: Make use of one of these statements:

Either:
(a) Select ‘carrid connid fldate price currency planetype’ into ‘table itab_flight from sflight’.
or
(b) Select * into corresponding fields of table ‘itab_flight’ from ‘sflight’.

(a) is better in performance than (b).

But before that, please take note of some performance related issues with OO Context.

1. When defining an Internal table, avoid occurring specification. It is obsolete, instead make use of Initial Size n.

2. Declare ‘Work area’ separately since Internal table is defined along with the header line being obsolete in OO Context. It’s better and more robust to fill the itab and fetch the values from itab using a separate ‘Work area’ rather than the header line. So, avoid header lines.

3. When defining an internal table, follow this way:
Define a Linetype (Field String) using the TYPES Statement:

```
TYPES: begin of ty_line,
```

```
f1 type i,
f2 type i,
end of ty_line.
```

Then, define a Table type using TYPES Statement:

```
TYPES: ty_lines type standard table of ty_line with
default key.
```

"There is difference between line and lines, so make it clear."

Then, define the internal table and its work area using a DATA statement as shown below:

```
DATA: i_lines type ty_lines,
wa_lines like line of i_lines
```

This is the standard way of defining the internal table under OO Context.

Your definition is creating a default header line that should be avoided.

Question 18: Checkboxes in ALV Output and table updating

I've made a report whose ALV output is as follows:

name skill rating handler reviewer

gp script 8
abc workflow 6

The handler and reviewer are 2 checkboxes. The user will click on the checkbox and make one person as handler and the other person as reviewer. After clicking the checkbox, when the user clicks on 'save' button, the data needs to be saved in a ztable.

I've done all the coding, but the problem is that after clicking the 'save' button, it's not recognized in the internal table when the checkbox was clicked. It's showing the old internal table in the debugging mode. If it can be recognized somehow, I can update my ztable.

What's the solution for this?

A: You can refer to the following example:

```
   loop at ls_outtab-celltab into ls_celltab.
        if ls_celltab-fieldname eq 'CHECKBOX'.
* §B4.Switch the style to dis- or enable a cell for
input
         if ls_celltab-style =
cl_gui_alv_grid=>mc_style_enabled.
          ls_celltab-style =
cl_gui_alv_grid=>mc_style_disabled.
         else.
          ls_celltab-style =
cl_gui_alv_grid=>mc_style_enabled.
         endif.
         modify ls_outtab-celltab from ls_celltab.
        endif.
      endloop.
      modify gt_outtab from ls_outtab index
es_row_no-row_id.
    call method sender->refresh_table_display.
From ex: BCALV_EDIT_05
```

You can also do it like the following:

```
    WHEN 'UPDATE'.

      DATA REF1 TYPE REF TO CL_GUI_ALV_GRID.
      CALL FUNCTION 'GET_GLOBALS_FROM_SLVC_FULLSCR'
           IMPORTING
                E_GRID = REF1.
      CALL METHOD REF1->CHECK_CHANGED_DATA.

      LOOP AT G_T_OUTTAB WHERE CHECK = 'X'.
" Update the Ztable
EnDLOOP:
```

Question 19: Checkboxes in ALV Output

I got an internal table as follows:

name skill rating
Gaurav Workflow 8
abc script 4
def ALV 5

I want to generate an ALV output of the above the internal table. I want to add 2 checkboxes like below in the ALV Output:

name skill rating handler reviewer
Gaurav Workflow 8 x
abc script 4 x
def ALV 5 x

In the above report, the output is as follows:

Gaurav is a handler of the ticket related to workflow.
abc is reviewer of the ticket related to script.
def is a handler of the ticket related to alv.

These checkboxes are not fixed. Anyone can be made reviewer and handler. One person can't play both roles simultaneously. This data will be saved in a z table.

I believe this can be handled through OOPS ALV.

What can be the coding for this?

Secondly, when the output list comes and the user selects the buttons after pressing the 'save' button, I want this data to be saved in the ztable.

How can I recognize which checkbox is clicked at the user command?

A: Add a field for check box in your itab, CHECK(1), and the field catalog for the field.

```
  L_FIELDCAT-INPUT    = 'X'.
  L_FIELDCAT-EDIT    = 'X'.
  L_FIELDCAT-CHECKBOX = 'X'.
```

For your second question, in the user command routine, use the following:

```
LOOP AT ITAB into wa_itab WHERE NOT CHECK IS INITIAL.
MODIFY ZTABLE FROM WA_ITAB.
ENDLOOP.
```

Question 20: ALV - OOPS Related Query

What is this class 'lcl_event_receiver' and its importing parameters (e_row e_column)?

In the class 'CL_GUI_ALV_GRID' (used to implement ALV Grids), there are some events defined to utilize some additional functionalities of the ALV Grid. For these types of functionalities, we require a class to be implemented (generally local in our program e.g. lcl_event_receiver in your program) to be the event handler for the ALV Grid instance.

The import parameters of the handler methods defined in the local class are basically nothing but the parameters of the events defined in global class 'CL_GUI_ALV_GRID'. So you can check it using SE24 transaction. Select the event and press "PARAMETERS" button to see what parameters the event have, and the same can be imported in the handler method of the event.

Question 21: ALV - access to protected method

I have an object from class "CL_GUI_ALV_GRID" and want to change the protected attribute "EVT_DELAYED_CHANGE_SELECTION Constant Protected" with the method:

```
CALL METHOD alv_grid->SET_DELAY_CHANGE_SELECTION
EXPORTING
time = lv_delay.
```

How can I access this protected attribute?

A: You could try to sub-class 'CL_GUI_ALV_GRID' and add a public method (e.g. SET_DELAY_CHANGE_SELECTION_PUBL) to your sub-class which will call the protected method.

Another suggestion is to define a sub-class inheriting the superclass, where the protected attributes and methods exist. Then you can access the protected methods and attributes.

Question 22: Bring 'Top_of_page' in OOPS ALV

Is there a sample coding to bring "Top_of_page" in OOPS ALV?

A: **One important thing is to split the screen into two parts using the splitter container and then use the first part to TOP_OF_PAGE and the second one to show the Grid data.**

Question 23: Node_Double_Click won't trigger ALV TREE

My class has an event that is triggered by (at least was supposed to be) 'Node_Double_Click'. I even tried 'Item_Double_Click' event and mark 'X' in 'item_selection' parameter when creating my instance of 'CL_GUI_ALV_TREE', but that event won't trigger too.

I already have set the handler (SET HANDLER me->event_name for r_alvtree) just right off the creating of the object (CL_GUI_ALV_TREE).

Then, I set the Method to be 'Event Handler', giving the name of the class 'CL_GUI_ALV_TREE' and 'Node_Double_Click' for the event (in detailed vision options).

I'm using Class Builder.

Still, have I missed something? When I tried to use another method like 'Header_Click', it works fine.

A: I assume you have not registered the event with the tree instance.

Have a look at the following sample report. The crucial parts are marked using $ADDED$:

(1) Register event with tree instance:

```
 "Register event for NODE_DOUBLE_CLICK
  l_event-eventid =
cl_gui_column_tree=>eventid_node_double_click.
  APPEND l_event TO lt_events.
```

(2) Set handler vor event:

```
  SET HANDLER l_event_receiver-
>handle_node_double_click

FOR tree1.
```

(3) Define and implement event handler method:

```
    METHODS handle_node_double_click
      FOR EVENT node_double_click OF cl_gui_alv_tree
        IMPORTING node_key.

ENDCLASS.                           "lcl_tree_event_receiver
DEFINITION
```

Question 24: Create ALV using Methods (oo)

How can I create ALV using Methods (oo)? Where do I go to start developing an ALV report?

A: Reports are created using SE38 or SE80 only.

For reference on OO ALV, check BCALV* reports in SE38. They are the best samples.

Question 25: Definition and use of ALV

What is ALV? What and where is it used?

A: The ALV Grid Control is a flexible tool for displaying lists. The tool provides common list operations as generic functions, and can be enhanced by self-defined options. This allows you to use the ALV Grid Control in a large range of application programs. In SAP development projects, the ALV Grid Control is also used as a tool for changing and creating tables.

Question 26: Disable some standard buttons from ALV display

I am creating an ALV display using object oriented approach. I know how to exclude some of the standard function buttons from the list.

But suppose instead of deleting, the requirement is to disable some standard buttons from ALV.

How can I do this?

A: You can go through the following steps:

1. Declare a handler method for the event TOOLBAR of class cl_gui_alv_grid.
2. For the above event, you will have 'e_object' as importing parameter.
3. In that 'e_object', you will have 'mt_toolbar' as an attribute which is an internal table.
4. In this internal table, you will have the details of all the buttons of the toolbar.
5. Loop that internal table with the ICON name and modify the field disabled = 'X'.

To disable some STD buttons, we need to pass an internal table with inactive functions in the method.

```
CALL METHOD MY_ALV->SET_TABLE_FOR_FIRST_DISPLAY
* IT_TOOLBAR_EXCLUDING =
```

Fill the internal table standard functions on an application tool bar that you want to hide.

Internal table must be of type ui_functions.
Use the constants of the class cl_gui_alv_grid to fill the field ui_func.

For example, you want to de-activate all the functions of the application tool bar, then insert cl_gui_alv_grid => mc_fc_excl_all into table <internal table name>.

Pass this internal table as parameter in the method set for first display.

Question 27: Displaying ALV tree in expanded form in the first ouput

I have a problem with ALV tree. My requirement is that on the first output itself the ALV tree should appear expanded depending on one of the filter criteria in the tool bar.

How can I trigger the toolbar event in PBO itself? Can it be done? If yes, please provide a sample code.

A: Yes, it can be done.

Question 28: Method Classification

What class does this method EXPAND_ALL exist?

A: It's the class CL_SALV_NODES.

You first have to get all the nodes:

```
nodes = gr_tree->get_nodes( ).
```

Then, call the expand method.

Question 29: Use of other methods

I found this method but I am not sure how to go ahead and use it. Can this method help me?

```
CL_PT_GUI_TMW_ALV_TREE->EXPAND_NODES
```

A: You can also try:

```
CALL METHOD tree->expand_root_nodes
EXPORTING level_count = level_count
expand_subtree = expand_subtree
EXCEPTIONS failed = 1
illegal_level_count = 2
cntl_system_error = 3.
```

Question 30: cl_gui_alv_tree

The class name of the tree I am using is cl_gui_alv_tree.

There is a method cl_gui_alv_tree->EXPAND_NODES in it, but I am not sure how to go ahead and use it. Will this one help?

A: Yes, that's it. You have to give the root node of your tree and set the parameter I_EXPAND_SUBTREE to true.

Question 31: Find next behavior in ALV container

I have an ALV grid in a custom container that's sized for a screen on a high-resolution tube. In other words, there's a scrollbar on the ALV but none on the screen itself (because the whole screen is visible at the high resolution).

At this high resolution, a 'find' or 'find next' will correctly scroll the ALV to the row in which an item is found (when the "found" row is below the currently visible row of the ALV).

But when I switch to a lower resolution where I have a scroll bar on the ALV and on the window itself, a 'find' or 'find next' does not scroll the ALV properly. You have to manually scroll to find the "found" row.

I have both resizings checked on the container.

Is there a way I can:

1) find the resolution the user is in?
2) modify the screen size to fit this resolution?
3) modify the container size to fit this resolution?

If I have a custom subscreen on top of the ALV, the re-sizing gets screwed up.

As soon as I commented out the call to the sub-screen in the flow logic, the problem disappeared.

What's happening in here?

A: If your container was placed on a screen painter, you can easily expand the screen to maximum values that you could have.

You can set the custom control attributes: check the box for re-sizing vertical and horizontal, and set the minimum lines and minimum columns to 1.

The second situation sounds like a GUI error. Make sure you have the latest patches for your SAP GUI.

Question 32: Problem in changing the layout of ALV to Excel

I have developed an ALV program, wherein I need to show the graphs for the same. For this, I need my data in Excel format so that I can write some macros and do further processing on it. I am using an appraoch I found on SDN "Report with graph".

I learned that I need SAP R/3: Add On:Interactive Excel. Even after installing it, I was unable to view the data in excel layout when I do "Change Layout->View->Microsoft Excel".

Is there another setting required to view the data in excel?

On the Excel side, we can change the security level (Tools->Macro->Security) to either low, medium, or high.

Is there any such provision in SAP?

A: Change the macro settings in your Excel sheet and then check if it works. Do the following:

-Open empty excel sheet

-In menu Tools-->Macros-->Security

-Change the radio button to medium

In the same pop-up, go to the second tab 'Trusted Publishers' and check the checkbox 'Trust access to visual basic project'.

Another suggestion is to check whether or not SAP R/3 AddOn: Interactive Excel is installed on your server. It may be possible that your colleague is working on a different server, and you are working on another server. So ask the BASIS people to install it on your server.

After that, when you run your program, on the ALV toolbar, there is a button called "Views".
In there, select "Excel Inplace". You should be able to view the data.

Question 33: Tree in OOPS ALV

How can I add a tree like structure of folder in a container which is the class and method for this?

What should be my concern in splitting a container?

A: Do not use split screen, instead use a docking container if it is your requirement.

```
* Docking Container
data docking type ref to cl_gui_docking_container.
* Picture Control
data picture type ref to cl_gui_picture.
* Definition of Control Framework
data  init.
data ok_code type sy-ucomm.
data repid type sy-repid.
data dynnr type sy-dynnr.

    repid = sy-repid.
    dynnr = sy-dynnr.
* create the docking container
    create object docking
                  exporting repid     = repid
                            dynnr     = dynnr
                            side      = docking-
>dock_at_left
                            extension = 180.
* create the picture container
    create object picture
                  exporting parent = docking.
```

Instead of creating picture control, create ALV here.

Question 34: Showing header for ALV tree

How can I show the header for ALV tree?

How can I use the method 'top_of_page OF cl_gui_alv_tree'?

A: Insert a design object with a table-type layout at the beginning of the ALV output:
. . .

Other Areas

Question 35: IDOCS

I have never worked upon IDOCS and ALEs and EDIs.

Is there any status codes I can refer to for debugging?

A: Some important status codes are as follows:

Inbound Status Codes

50 Error --> It will go for ALE Service Layer

56 Error --> Idoc with Errors added

51 Error --> Application Document not posted

65 Error --> Error in ALE Service Layer

For 51 or 56 errors, do the following steps:
goto WE19 --> give the IDOC Number and Execute-->
Press on Inbound function Module

for 65 Error --> goto SE38 --> Execute the Program RBDAPP01 then you're getting 51 Error.

Question 36: Transporting Segments and IDOC

I have created a segment type and an IDOC extension type. I need to transport it to another client.

How can I transport the segment?

Which one has to be transported first, is it the segment or the IDOC?

A: It is always better to keep both the changes related to segment and idoc extension in the same request. If they are in separate request, first transport the request related to the segment and then the IDOC extension request. Release the segment and then the IDOC extension.

Another suggestion is to save the segment and idoc extenstion in one request. If not, move the segment first and the Idoc extension next.

If you face another problem, create a new package and include all your objects (idoc extension and segements) into one transport. Then, you don't have to worry about the sequence.

Question 37: Invoice Idoc - user exit

I have a requirement in the user exit in Invoice idoc.

I have identified the user exit 'EXIT_SAPLVEDF_002'.
The Idoc is 'INVOIC02'.
I need to work on the segment 'E1EDK01'.
The include is ZXEDFU02.

My requirements are the following:

1. I have to add 'vsart_bez and augru_bez' fields to the idoc segment.

2. Then, I have to populate 'LIKP_TRATY' (Means of Transport type) with 'Vsart_bez',
and populate the Header text with 'Augru_bez'.

How can I check the user exit for invoice idoc?

How can I check the changes made?

More over I need to populate the segment 'E1EDK01', fields 'VSART_BEZ', and 'AUGRU_BEZ' using the exit. I need to check if the idoc is carrying the data correctly or not.

How can I do that?

A: To get custom fields on IDOC, you need to add a custom segment on IDOC. For that, you have to create an extension IDOC with reference to Basic IDOC.

You can do that as explained below.

For example, you have a basic idoc ORDERS05 and you want to add additional segments at header level - ZE1EDK01 and line item level ZE1EDP01.

1. TCode - WE31: Create custom segments ZE1EDK01 and ZE1EDP01 with the fields you want and release these segments.

2. TCode - WE30 : Create extension IDOC.

In WE20, enter extension IDOC name - ZORDERS05, select "Extension" option and hit "create" button. When it gives pop-up, select "create new" and enter linked basis type as "ORDERS05". Enter proper description and save.

3. On the next screen of WE30, select the segment under which you want to add your additional segment. Save everything.

4. TCode - WE82. Here, you link extension idoc to basic idoc and message type.
Go into change mode. Hit "New entries button". Enter Message type = "ORDERS", basic type = "ORDERS05" and extension type = "ZORDERS05".

You can populate this segment and the fields you want using the user-exit available in that particular IDOC processing.

Some common user-exits are:

1. Purchase Order IDOC: ORDERS05
Enhancement: MM06E001 - User exits for EDI inbound and outbound purchasing documents.

2. Quotation IDOC: ORDERS05
Enhancement: VEDE0001 - SD EDI Outbound quotation (customer enhancement).

3. Invoice IDOC (bill. doc): INVOIC02
Enhancement: LVEDF001 - User exit for IDOC_OUTPUT_INVOICE.

Question 38: Trigger User Exit

In the client system, I have created the segments YE1EDK01 . The Message type is INVOIC.

I have also created an Object Type - Extension Zinvoic02.

I have the user exit LVEDF001 and the function module EXIT_SAPLVEDF_002.

If I keep a debugger in the user exit, when will it get triggered?

Now, we have the extension type ZINVOIC02. Will it reflect in the standard Invoice Idoc?
If it does, how can I check that?

I have added 2 segments now. I have to populate those fields using 'vsart_bez' and 'augru_bez'.

A: Keep the break point at the user exit. Create invoice or change invoice (vf01 or vf02) when you maintain the output type in invoice.

Now, click on further data ->select periodic scheduling-> back and save it.

Run 'RSNAST00' Program.

Output application: V3
Object key: Invoice number
Output type: RD00 Medium = 6(EDI), A (ALE)

When you execute the program, it will go to debugging.

Then you can see what values are coming. Another suggestion is to check if you have activated CMOD and SMOD.

Only the debug will go to your user exit. Make sure all SMOD-->components are green.

Question 39: Fetch Data from an Object

This is a requirement in a BADI. The BADI is triggered by some program and it has an Object 'ct_valid_lanes' as an Input Parameter.

The Object 'ct_valid_lanes' is of type "ANY TABLE". By debugging, I found out that it has many fields say MATNR, MATID, LOCNO, etc. and has more than one data for each field.

I want to fetch these data from the object and put it into my internal table. I can't loop at an object and also I don't know how to read fields in an object.

How can I do these?

A: You can do all those things using Field-Symbols.

Question 40: CRM BADI ORDER_SAVE

Since no documentation exists on most of the CRM Badi's, I am a bit in the dark about using these. This ORDER_SAVE is what I want to use, but I have some issues.

I want to check an authorization object on the ACTIVITY REASON drop-down field. So inside my BADI implementation METHOD CHECK_ACTIVITY_REASON, I call a function module to get the chosen activity reason and check the authorization object. If SY-SUBRC is NE 0, I then want to issue an error message to the user and NOT let the transactions SAVE but RETURNED to the screen for USER input again.

How do I use the fields CV_OWN_MESSAGE and raise the exception DO_NOT_SAVE to fulfill my purpose?

Secondly, I have another problem where the BADI CRM_ORDER_FIELDCHECK is activated and stops after this message. Here, we check this activity reason and set it to 'not changeable'. So the user, after getting the error message cannot change the reason. I manage to overcome this problem by setting a MEMORY-ID as a marker after the error is issued in the ORDER SAVE BADI, and then overcome this in the CRM_ORDER_FIELDCHECK by importing this MEMORYID and check for the marker to avoid changing the reason to NOT CHANGEABLE. I am only concerned that in a call center with a few thousand users, this memory id might cause a problem. Apparently, the memory id's works per session. Any ideas?

A: You only have to mark the field 'CV_OWN_MESSAGE', and after that call the sentence 'MESSAGE ...' with the addition 'RAISING do_not_save'. It's something like this:

```
AUTHORITY-CHECK OBJECT 'ZOBJECT'
ID 'ACTVT' FIELD '97'.
IF sy-subrc <> 0.
cv_own_message = 'X'.
MESSAGE e000(zorder) WITH text-001 text-002 RAISING
do_not_save.
ENDIF.
```

I used it in the PREPARE method in the ORDER_SAVE BAdI, and it works really well.

For your second query, the documentation says this about SET/GET PARAMETER ID:

* The global user-related SAP memory is available to each user for the entire duration of a terminal session. For this reason, set values are retained when you leave a program.
* You should not use SAP memory for temporary storage because a user's parallel sessions use the same global memory.

Then you will not have problems with that few thousand users. The only problem comes with the second point, if they open two sessions (here is where I trust them, because I think they will never open two sessions and work in two projects at the same time) It also depends on the client and his job. You must be sure you initialize the PARAMETER ID in all cases, which isn't always easy to do.

Question 41: BAPI return parameter

I am working in version ECC 6.0. I want to create a BAPI for one of our requirement. For that, I have created one function module. In that function module, it has an import parameter and the output goes in table parameter. I have also declared export parameter as "RETURN TYPE BAPIRETURN". The function is executing as expected.

When I am trying to add this function as API method in SWO1 transaction, it gives me an error like 'BAPI &1: BAPI function module & 2 has no return parameter'.

How can I deal with the error?

What is the meaning of the procedure?

How can I define the reference of the BOR parameters to the function module parameter in the BOR?

This is the error message that I received:

"BAPI: BAPI function module ZBAPI_BOM_READ1 has no return parameter
Message no. S&537".

Diagnosis

The system checks that the RETURN parameter has been defined in both the BOR and in the function module. The parameter must refer to one of the BAPI return structures (all planned reference structures can be used for BAPIs up to and including Release 4.6B; but from Release 4.6C only BAPIRET2 can be used).

The BOR parameter must be type EXPORT (one line or multi-line) and the function module parameter must be type EXPORT (if one line) or type TABLE (if multi-line).

Procedure

Create a RETURN parameter for the function module. Also define the reference of the BOR parameters to the function module parameter in the BOR ("Name in function module").

A: Change that return parameter to 'TABLES parameter' from 'EXPORT parameter', and make it 'Non-optional' or 'mandatory parameter'.

Meanwhile, the structure of your BAPI return table does not match with BOR.

Check whether you have given relevant structure to your return table. The return table parameter should be of structure BAPIRET2.

Put return parameters as TABLE PARAMETER AND mark optional. If not, just check with the useful BAPI's you have come accross with this development.

The reason for the error is the created function name started with ZBAPI. Actually, it should start with BAPI only.

Question 42: Error while creating Sales Order using BAPI

I'm trying to use "BAPI_SALESORDER_CREATEFROMDAT1" to create Sales Order.

It gave 'Error in creating document'. I'm unable to figure what I'm missing.

Did I give the wrong parameters?

How can I determine what the return error is?

A: All the data that was given to the 'Salesorder' while creating sales order in normal transaction needs to be filled when calling the BAPI.

You need to verify all the data including the ones automatically filled and the mandatory data is passed to the BAPI.

To see the exact error, include the following coding:

```
loop at return.
write : / return-type,
return-id,
return-number,
return-message,
return-message_v1,
return-message_v2,
return-message_v3,
return-message_v4.
endloop.
```

Another analysis is the return table contains all the messages due to errors that similarly would occur in the dialogue transaction. Because BAPI's are usually called via RFC, they collect errors and do not raise any exception. Otherwise, the RFC connection would break down.

Thus, look carefully through the E-messages in the return table.

Question 43: SO is having multiple items

I was able to track the error and it was due to wrong data.

If my SO is having multiple items, then what changes do I need to do?

Do I need to use "BAPI_SALESDOCU_CREATEFROMDATA2"?

What's the difference between "BAPI_SALESDOCU_CREATEFROMDATA1" and "BAPI_SALESDOCU_CREATEFROMDATA2"?

A: For multiple line items, you have to append the same in the table "ORDER_ITEMS_IN", in "ORDER_ITEMS_INX", and in the schedule lines related table.

Question 44: Additional code for Sales Order Creation

I'm using the following code to try to create a sales order, but the order is not bein created. What is the problem?

```
* Line item number.
item-itm_number = '000010'.
itemx-itm_number = 'X'.

* Material
item-material = p_matnr.
itemx-material = 'X'.

* Plant
item-plant = p_plant.
itemx-plant = 'X'.

* Quantity
item-target_qty = p_menge.
itemx-target_qty = 'X'.

APPEND item.
APPEND itemx.

* For second item.

* Line item number.
item-itm_number = '000020'.
itemx-itm_number = 'X'.

* Material
item-material = '600020001'.
itemx-material = 'X'.

* Plant
item-plant = p_plant.
itemx-plant = 'X'.

* Quantity
item-target_qty = p_menge.
itemx-target_qty = 'X'.

APPEND item.
APPEND itemx.


* Fill schedule lines
lt_schedules_in-itm_number = '000010'.
lt_schedules_in-sched_line = '0001'.
lt_schedules_in-req_qty = p_menge.
APPEND lt_schedules_in.
```

```
* Fill schedule lines
lt_schedules_in-itm_number = '000020'.
lt_schedules_in-sched_line = '0002'.
lt_schedules_in-req_qty = p_menge.
APPEND lt_schedules_in.

* Fill schedule line flags
lt_schedules_inx-itm_number = '000010'.
lt_schedules_inx-sched_line = '0001'.
lt_schedules_inx-updateflag = 'X'.
lt_schedules_inx-req_qty = 'X'.
APPEND lt_schedules_inx.

* Fill schedule line flags
lt_schedules_inx-itm_number = '000020'.
lt_schedules_inx-sched_line = '0002'.
lt_schedules_inx-updateflag = 'X'.
lt_schedules_inx-req_qty = 'X'.
APPEND lt_schedules_inx.
```

But I guess it's overwriting my frst material.

I'm also getting the error: "For object rv_beleg, number range interval does not exist".

What can I do to finally resolve this?

A: If you initially create your sales order, there is no need to fill the change-indicator structures (e.g. ITEMX).

If there are higher "versions" of the BAPI that are available in your system (e.g. BAPI_SALESDOCU_CREATEFROMDATA2), then go for this BAPI.

Finally, if you experience problems with certain document types (BAPI does not create them), then you can use the underlying RFC-enabled function module SD_SALESDOCUMENT_CREATE directly. If you look at the coding of 'BAPI_SALESDOCU_CREATEFROMDATA2', it calls fm 'SD_SALESDOCUMENT_CREATE' with IMPORTING parameter:
BUSINESS_OBJECT = 'BUS2032';

Question 45: Controlling objects

How can I restrict the number of objects to be created for a class?

How can we do it for standard classes?

A: In the constructor method, increment a static attribute, keep a check on its value, and display the message accordingly.

Another suggestion is to keep a static attribute for the class, say class A, to keep a count of the number of objects and increment in the contructor. Also, make the constructor private. In a friend class, say class B, instatiate the class A and always check the count variable and do not instantiate the class if it exceeds the maximum desired value.

We need a friend class to increment static variable in the constructor and check its value before instantiating the class.

You can change CONSTRUCTOR method of the global class in SE24 and then do the check in your program.

For standard classes, it's really not possible to restrict the number of objects strictly as they might not even have a static attribute to count the number of objects instantiated. What you can do is keep a variable locally in your program and before you instantiate the class, check if the value is greater than or equal to the maximum value desired. Increment the value after instantiation.

You can also consider the following two cases:

1. For one program context, you need to restrict the number of instances of a global class.

It is possible. Use the method I had suggested earlier.

2. Irrespective of the program context, you need to restrict the number of instances of a global class.
For this case, you can try using PERSISTENT classes to store the objects of the class persistently.

Question 46: Save object in memory

I have to save an instance in memory because I need the information later.

The program goes like this:

1) Get instance1.
2) Call sap-classes and methods.
3) Create instance2.
4) Call function to show instance2.
5) Start BDT functions. (At this point, I lose my information about instance1)

How can I write the instance1 into "global memory" for accessing all data all the time?

A: Shared Memory Objects is a new concept implemented in NetWeaver 2004, and enhanced in NetWeaver 7.0.

If your application is using BDT, then you can use 'BDT_INSTANCE_SELECT' with pop option. You can use push and pop to push one instance and pop the other one.

You can also try to serialize the instance to write it to a string in XML format and export/import this string and deserialize.

Another suggestion if you want to save an instance of a class in memory, you can use persistent classes.

Generally, ABAP programs work with data and objects that are valid at runtime. They are transient i.e. temporary and disappear when program ends.

To store this data permanently and independently of the program context, i.e. persistently, it must be stored in the database. This means instances of global classes can be written to database tables.

Persistent Services in ABAP Objects can be used to write the current attribute values of objects defined as persistent to associated transparent tables. On request, these values can be imported from the tables and assigned to an object previously

defined as persistent.
To use persistent services for objects, their types must be created as persistent classes in Class Builder.

You can also try the following statement:

```
EXPORT P_DATUM to MEMORY id 'G_DATUM'.
```

In other coding:
```
IMPORT (from memory id)
```

Question 47: Business Objects

Where do we use Business objects?

How do I find the BAPI or Function module tied to any specific method of a BO?

How do I call the BAPI in my program?

A: Business objects in R/3 are nothing more than documentation. For example, in SWO1, the business object for Sales Orders describes attributes and methods of the sales orders. The methods of the object are usually tied to BAPIs or function modules. These are the programming objects that you can use in your program.

For example, go to transaction SWO1, enter 'BUS2032' and click 'display'. This is the BO for sales order. You can now see a tree structure, open the 'methods node' (lets say that we want to create a sales order), double click on the method 'SalesOrder.CreateFromData2'. This is the newest version of this method. You'll see in the dialog a tab for 'ABAP', click this. You will see the name of the BAPI here. In order to call this BAPI in your programs, you can simply use the 'Patturn' button in the editor for call function modules. Enter the BAPI name and click 'green check mark'. Of course, you will have to pass certain things to the BAPI.

Question 48: Create object

I am creating an object with reference to a class.

```
data:        g_custom_container type ref to
cl_gui_custom_container,

create object g_custom_container
                  exporting container_name =
'CUST_CONT'.
```

What is the parameter CONTAINER_NAME for? I cannot see that parameter in the class.

What is the explanation for this?

A: Have a look at the sample report 'BCALV_GRID_DEMO'. The container name is the name of the custom control on the dynpro where you want to display your ALV list. This way you "attach" your container instance to this custom control element on the screen.

Another suggestion is to go in se24 to display "cl_gui_custom_container" and see the signature of the CONSTRUCTOR method. The 'container_name' is "Name of the dynpro CustCtrl name to link this container to".

You first have to define in your DYNPRO a custom container with the SCREEN PAINTER and give it a name, for example 'CUST_CONT'. Then, you create the object and can use it (for example to display a grid).

A container name is a parameter in constructor of 'cl_gui_custom_container class'. It holds the name of the 'custom control' which you have pasted on the screen, and this in turn holds the ALV grid at run time.

So when you create an instance of 'cl_gui_custom_container', it asks for the parameter 'container_name'. Give the name of the custom control you have pasted in your screen.

Question 49: Client dependent objects in ABAP/SAP

What are client dependent objects in abap/sap?

A: Client dependent objects can be found in SAP Scripts and tables.

Client independent objects can be found in Smartforms, programs, and function modules.

If an Object is Client dependent, then it cannot be found in another client even in the same server. For example, if an event is created fro a Workflow Object, it would be Client dependent and you have created it in Dev Client 100, and your testing client is Dev 120. Now the event which you have used to trigger the workflow would not be found in Client DEV120, unless or othewise you transport to the testing client.

If an Object is Client Independent, then it would be available in all the clients of that particular server. For example, you created a report program in SE38 in Client DEV 100 and then you have to test it in Client DEV 120. In this case, the program you have created will be available in Client DEV 120 and transport to that client is not required.

Objects that are stored in 'Customizing Request' are Client dependent and objects stored in Workbench Request are Client independent.

Question 50: Object released

How and by whom the object is released and transported?

Which will transfer to the 'quality server' from the development server?

A: Whoever has the authorization (Team members/Team leader) to release the Task and the Request, that person will release the request. Then the BASIS people will import the request in the desired system, and then the 'Object' will be available in the target system.

It also depends on your project. Most of the time, the developer will release the request from development to 'Quality' by using Se10 or Se09 transaction. Once you're done, then you need to import the object to 'Quality' by STMS Transaction.

Try to enter 'development system' and 'Se10 transaction', and if you are able to view it then you'll have the authorization. The same thing with log on 'quality system' and enter STMS transaction, and if you are able to see STMS then you'll have the authorization.

Another explanation is the transport request is created and in that, tasks are created for developers. Developers code and save the object under the task and release tasks in SE10.

Once all tasks are released, the creator of transport request will release the request in SE10. After that, basis people will transport request to another server.

Question 51: Function Module versus Object Oriented Programming (OOP's)

I was recently thinking about why I should use Function Modules when I can as well work with OOPs concept. Can we do without the Function Module?

In which scenarios should we prefer a Function Module and why?

Are Function Modules redundant going forward? Or are there places we would still need Function Modules? If yes, can you please kindly let me know in which scenarios?

A: You are correct but SAP is introducing OOPs concept recently, where as there are lot of pre-defined function modules existing from the beginning. So instead of writing the code again with OOPs, it's better to go with the existing function module's rite.

It saves a lot of time. Not only that those are SAP provided standard function modules, you will not get many problems.

As quoted from SAP help:

"From Function Groups to Objects

At the center of any object-oriented model are objects, which contain attributes (data) and methods (functions). Objects should enable programmers to map a real problem and its proposed software solution on a one-to-one basis. Typical objects in a business environment are, for example, 'customer', 'Order', or 'Invoice'. From Release 3.1 onwards, the Business Object Repository (BOR) has contained examples of such objects. The object model of ABAP Objects, the object-oriented extension of ABAP, is compatible with the object model of the BOR.

Before R/3 Release 4.0, the nearest equivalent of objects in ABAP were function modules and function groups. Suppose we have a function group for processing orders. The attributes of an order correspond to the global data of the function group, while the individual function modules represent actions that manipulate that data (methods). This means that the actual order data is encapsulated in the function group, and is never directly addressed, but instead only through the function modules. In this way, the function modules can ensure that the data is consistent.

When you run an ABAP program, the system starts a new internal session. The internal session has a memory area that contains the ABAP program and its associated data. When you call a function module, an instance of its function group plus its data, is loaded into the memory area of the internal session. An ABAP program can load several instances by calling function modules from different function groups."

The instance of a function group in the memory area of the internal session almost represents an object in the sense of object orientation. (See also the definition in the section What is Object Orientation?.. When you call a function module, the calling program uses the instance of a function group, based on its description in the Function Builder. The program cannot access the data in the function group directly, but only through the function module. The function modules and their parameters are the interface between the function group and the user. The main difference between real object orientation and function groups is that although a program can work with the instances of several function groups at the same time, it cannot work with several instances of a single function group. Suppose a program wanted to use several independent counters, or process several orders at the same time. In this case, you would have to adapt the function group to include instance administration, for example, by using numbers to differentiate between the instances.

In practice, this is very awkward. Consequently, the data is usually stored in the calling program, and the function modules are called to work with it (structured programming). One problem is, for example, that all users of the function module must use the same data structures as the function group itself. Changing the internal data structure of a function group affects many users, and it is often difficult to predict the implications. The only way to avoid this is to rely heavily on interfaces and a technique that guarantees that the internal structures of instances will remain hidden, allowing you to change them later without causing any problems.

This requirement is met by object orientation. ABAP Objects allows you to define data and functions in classes instead of function groups. Using classes, an ABAP program can work with any number of instances (objects) based on the same template.

Instead of loading a single instance of a function group into memory implicitly when a function module is called, the ABAP program can now generate the instances of classes explicitly using the new ABAP statement CREATE OBJECT. The individual instances represent unique objects. You address these using object references. The object references allow the ABAP program to access the interfaces of the instances.

The following sections contain more information about classes, objects, interfaces, and object references in ABAP Objects.

Another suggestion for this is when there's a need of a functionality where I believe the SAP standard provides this "service" (either as function module or class method), I look first for class methods and then for function modules.

In many cases, the classes are more powerful and versatile than the corresponding function modules.

An example for this is for reading a time sheet data (table CATSDB), we can use either
- BAPI BAPI_CATIMESHEETRECORD_GETLIST or the
- class CL_DBSEL_CATS.

Selection Criteria
The BAPI allows the following selection criteria:
- FROMDATE, TODATE, employees

The CONSTRUCTOR method of class CL_DBSEL_CATS has the following interface:
IM_CALLING_PROGRAM Calling Program
IM_AUTHORITY_CHECK_TYPE Authorization Check R=Reporting, E=Change, D=Approve
IM_FIELD_SELECTION Field Names for DB Seln. Corresponds to GET CATSDB FIELDS ..
IM_SELECTION_CRITERIA Selection Criteria for CATSDB Selection
IM_FREE_SELECTIONS Free Selections for Database Fields
IM_BADI BADI for Customer Enhancements

Thus, we can either define multiple selection criteria of our own (using parameters IM_SELECTION_CRITERIA and IM_FREE_SELECTIONS), or we can "link" the selection screen of a report to this class (IM_CALLING_PROGRAM). In addition, parameter IM_BADI further allows us to modify the selection if necessary.

Authorization Checks

The BAPI strictly checks for 'Reporting' authorization, whereas the class allows us to define different authorization levels (using parameter IM_AUTHORITY_CHECK_TYPE: Authorization Check R=Reporting, E=Change, D=Approve).

Messages

If the user does not have 'Reporting' authorization, the BAPI simply skips the record:

```
...
  LOOP AT ICATSDB.
    MOVE SY-TABIX TO L_TABIX.
    CALL FUNCTION 'CATS_CHECK_AUTHORITY'
         EXPORTING
              PERNR            = ICATSDB-PERNR
              DATE             = ICATSDB-WORKDATE
              ACTION           = 'R'
         EXCEPTIONS
              PERNR_NOT_FOUND = 1
              INVALID_ACTION  = 2
              NO_AUTHORITY    = 3
              OTHERS          = 4.
    IF SY-SUBRC <> 0.
      CONTINUE.
    ENDIF.
...
```

In contrast, method GET_REJECT_COUNT returns the number of records skipped due to authorization problems.

I hope you will understand now why it is worth to spend some time and search for the most appropriate classes to realize out applications.

If you are writing any custom functionality for your requirement, the existing methods are not enough to give solutions. In that case, you will introduce FM. In that, you can use classes and methods.

You should understand that apparently Function Groups and classes are somewhat similar.

Function Groups - > Data + Function Modules
Class -> Data + Methods

Both support encapsulation i.e. data (if defined as private in class) can only be accessed by the methods/function modules of class/function group.

But the area in use of class and function group is different. If you need to simulate a real life scenario wherein you require creating several runtime instances of a real world entity, then we cannot use Function groups and have to use classes because class has the property of multiple instantiation.

But if you need to deal with only one instance, then you can use Function group.

It is very important to design an object oriented solution and see if it is at all required before writing a piece of code in an object oriented manner.

On the other hand, OO is really easy. All you need to do in your program is just instantiate the object (assuming an Instance type method/attribute) and then you will get all the data.

If you need extra methods or attributes, you can just define a subclass inheriting everything from the main class. So, you only need to add your method/attribute coding.

It's a lot easier in any case to code in an ABAP this sort of stuff:

```
* Instantiate our Sales order from parameter
data : obj type ref to zcl_sales_order. "Ref to class
create object obj exporting vbeln = p_vbeln.
* attributes of Sales Order class
assign obj->partners to <g_partners>. "Partner addresses
assign obj->positions to <g_positions>. "Line items
assign obj->v_vbeln to <g_salesdoc>. "Sales Doc number
assign obj->materials to <g_materials>. "Material list
assign obj->docflow to <g_documents>. "Document flow
```

rather than mess around with function modules. The code within the method is totally separate from the caller as well.

If I have several sales orders (multiple instances), I can still use the same code by just instantiating the sales order class (create object xxx). Then to get attributes/methods, I can use exactly the same code on the new object (Multiple instances).

Function modules are not designed to be handled by multiple instances. Function modules are OK when you are dealing with a single instance and the code isn't too complex. Also for a while, SAP has a load of function modules for which classes aren't available yet, but this will change in the near future.

Now if I need some other data, for example say invoices for orders, I can just add a method using most of the data I've already got from the existing class (inheritance). In other words, a new class can refer to to an existing class as a "Super Class".

Polymorphism is also another extremely powerful OO concept where you can have identically named methods which behave differently in different classes. In other words, you can have the same method in different child classes but each with a different implementation.

Both the above concepts allows for code re-use and drastically cut the development time, provided the class structure has been properly thought out and implemented.

Also, the scope for programming errors is very much reduced. Coding time is cut significantly as you now only need to worry about the actual business function.

Now, all you need to do in the application program is to instantiate an object, define some event handlers, get the attributes or call any relevant methods, and produce any required output.

Using a Function Module, I'd probably have to re-read a whole slew of data I've already got from the Sales Order Attributes anyway.
(Business objects -- transaction SWO1) were a sort of start to OO ABAP, but genuine classes are the way forward even in workflow scenarios (rel 6.40 and up).

If you've ever used SWO1 in TEST mode, you can see that

Business objects also had a load of useful functionality but weren't actually used so much in ordinary ABAP. OO actually deprecate a lot of the business object stuff.

SE24 in test mode gives a similar output to SWO1.

Question 52: Cannot create object

I have the following code:

```
DATA: ref_cl_rsd_odso TYPE REF TO cl_rsd_odso,
ref_if_rsd_dta type ref to if_rsd_dta,
e_s_dta TYPE rsd_s_dta,
wa_e_s_dta TYPE rsd_s_dta.


START-OF-SELECTION.

create object ref_cl_rsd_odso.

CALL METHOD ref_cl_rsd_odso->if_rsd_dta~dta_get_info
IMPORTING
e_s_dta = e_s_dta.
```

It returns an activation error:

"You cannot create an instance of the class "CL_RSD_ODSO" outside the class".

How can I fix this?

A: I think there's no need to create an instance for this class.

Then, the code will be:

```
DATA: ref_cl_rsd_odso TYPE REF TO cl_rsd_odso,
ref_if_rsd_dta type ref to if_rsd_dta,
e_s_dta TYPE rsd_s_dta,
wa_e_s_dta TYPE rsd_s_dta.


START-OF-SELECTION.


CALL METHOD ref_cl_rsd_odso->if_rsd_dta~dta_get_info
IMPORTING
e_s_dta = e_s_dta.
```

The class "cl_rsd_odso" has its instantiation set to 'Private' which means that you cannot create a public instance of the same in your program. The class can only be instantiated from within itself.

Your program should work if you comment out the 'Create object' statement.

If you want to create an object of that class, declare a static method in that class. Call that method using the syntax "class_name=>method_name" in the start-of-selection, and then create the object in that method.

Question 53: "create object"

If I comment "create object", the activation is ok. But there is a dump when
run pgm (OBJECTS_OBJREF_NOT_ASSIGNED, CX_SY_REF_IS_INITIAL).

Is there a solution for this?

A: We need to call the factory method to get the instance of this class.

```
DATA: ref_cl_rsd_odso TYPE REF TO cl_rsd_odso,
ref_if_rsd_dta type ref to if_rsd_dta ,
e_s_dta TYPE rsd_s_dta,
wa_e_s_dta TYPE rsd_s_dta.


START-OF-SELECTION.


CALL METHOD CL_RSD_ODSO=>FACTORY
* EXPORTING
* I_ODSOBJECT = SPACE
* I_REFNM =
* I_TXTLG =
* I_TXTSH =
* I_INFOAREA =
* I_BWAPPL =
RECEIVING
R_R_ODSO = ref_cl_rsd_odso.
* EXCEPTIONS
* INPUT_INVALID = 1
* CANCELLED = 2
* others = 3
.
IF SY-SUBRC <> 0.
* MESSAGE ID SY-MSGID TYPE SY-MSGTY NUMBER SY-MSGNO
* WITH SY-MSGV1 SY-MSGV2 SY-MSGV3 SY-MSGV4.
ENDIF.

CALL METHOD ref_cl_rsd_odso->if_rsd_dta~dta_get_info
IMPORTING
e_s_dta = e_s_dta.
```

Question 54: Infotype 21

I'm uploading the infotype 21 (family details) through function module 'hr_infotype_operations'. I found that infotype 0106 (family/related person) is a secondary infotype and that a record is created for 0106 everytime you create a record in 21. So, I uploaded the family data of an employee using the function module for infotype 21 initially, and then fetch the same record from the table pa0106 and modify the same record with other information.

For example, I have the address details of a dependent (father subtype 11) in infotype 21. This address data is stored in the table pa0106. I'm not able to modify the record for infotype 0106 using the function module 0106.

What can be the reason for this? Is it because that infotype 0106 is a secondary infotype and you cannot modify the record using the FN module?

A: Check the RETURN table of that FM if you are getting any errors.

You need to specify the secondary infotype table for this parameter.

Question 55: Data of infotype 0031

In what table data of infotype 0031 is saved?

I checked it in pa0031 and it is empty.

A: Infotype 0031 is stored in table PA0031. If the table is supposed to hold data, then you should see it in transaction PA30 (choosing infotype 0031).

There is a standard function that does all what it's doing, bringing this data 'HR_READ_0031_DB'.

Question 56: User Input as an Excel File

I want to create a program where it will ask the user to give an Excel file. After that, whatever data contents are in there, it has to be transferred into an internal table for further processing.

How is that possible?

A: See the example program. This program upload excel file as an input and upload the data into an internal table. From the internal table, it updates the database table.

Question 57: Problem while trying to execute Excel macro

I'm currently opening an excel document stored within BDS, and I'm trying to populate certain fields before running a macro.

When I was previously using OLE objects to do this, I managed to do this as well as run the macro which was responsible to print a relevant sheet in Excel.

However, as I'm now required to read the document from BDS, I'm using the 'I_OI_DOCUMENT_PROXY' class to run the Excel macro. I've tried using the 'EXECUTE_MACRO' method but I keep getting the error 'MACRO_OR_SCRIPT_FAILED'.

What's the cause of this and how do I go about solving this?

A: As the macro was created within a module, when calling the 'EXECUTE_MACRO' method, the module name would have to be specified first and followed by the actual macro name. Below is an example:

```
data: doc TYPE REF TO i_oi_document_proxy.

CALL METHOD doc->execute_macro
EXPORTING
macro_string = 'ModPrint.PrintCard'.
```

Where 'ModPrint' is the module and 'PrintCard' is the macro.

Question 58: Create graphic in MS-Excel with DOI

Is it possible to create graphics within the document because of DOI?

A: Check ABAP code sample generating graphs on excel using OLE. You can also check out report SAPRDEMOEXCELINTEGRATION2.

Question 59: Handling mandatory import parameters

How can I handle the check for initial status of the import parameters which are not optional?

I do not need my method call to proceed without supplying some input (not inital) for the import parameters.

If exceptions are the only way to handle it, I would like to see one sample code for the same.

A: In the method parameters, you can define the exception code like 'NO_INPUT'.

In the code of the method, check the parameter.

Example:
```
IF IM_INPUT IS INITIAL.

* Raise an exception that there is no input supplied.
  RAISE NO_INPUT.
ENDIF.
```

Without supplying the mandatory IMPORT parameter, you will get a SYNTAX error. So if you want to check in the program if the supplied parameter is not initial, then you have to check in the method implementation and raise an exception.

Example:

If IM_DATA is initial, raise exception type
cx_no_data_supplied (If class based exception. Recommended).

Also, you can use:
raise no_data_supplied.

Question 60: The F.M: NUMBER_GET_NEXT

What is the use of the Function Module:
NUMBER_GET_NEXT?

A: Check the doc is SE37 which is available in EN.

This FM will get the next N° of a document in its range.

For example, it enables to know the next number which will be attach to the next Sales Order.

It retrieves the last order N° created and increment it.

Question 61: Methods implemented

In our system, I found class. In t-code SE24, some of its method names are displayed in blue fonds, instead of ordinary black fonds. When I double click on the method names, a pop-up window indicates "Method xxx is implemented in class yyy". I have no idea about the relationship between the original class and the class yyy.

What can be the explanation for this?

A: In SE24, you find both 'Classes and Interfaces' that have methods in it. You might be clicking on a method of an interface, that's why it is showing like that.

Since methods of an interface are to be implemented in other class (as they are Abstract methods) you will not find the implementation of that method in that interface. The method will be implemented in some other class which implements that interface.

Another possibility is SE24 contains different type of classes in which ABSTRACT CLASSES contains at least one abstract method. I think whatever method you selecte, the type will be ABSTRACT methods. We can provide the implementation part for the abstract methods in its inherited class.

If you display class "CL_GUI_ALV_GRID" in transaction SE80 and open the folder "Methods", you will see which method will be displayed in "blue":
- All methods in the sub-folder 'Inherited Methods' are shown in blue.
- Some of these inherited methods have been redefined within the class (folder Redefinitions) and are displayed in "ordinary" black font.

To know the superclass of "CL_GUI_ALV_GRID" just display the 'Properties' tab strip of the class. There, you see that "CL_GUI_ALV_GRID_BASE" is the superclass.

Thus, all methods displayed in blue are methods inherited from the superclass that have not been redefined.

Question 62: Creating class and methods

I want to create a class and a method using se24.

How can I accomplish this?

A: Use The Web Design API for Tables enables you to modify individual cell data in relation to content, display and navigation options. To do this, you create your own ABAP class that inherits the associated properties and parameters from the class CL_RSR_WWW_MODIFY_TABLE and you redefine one or more methods for this class.

Question 63: Changing methods or read-only attributes

I have to call a method to change the 'NR'.
call METHOD go_specific->SET_NR

The method itself checks if I am in activity mode 01. I'm in 03 but I want to change the value.

Can I change the coding from the method order or can I simply change the 'md_activity' variable?

A: It would depend on what is allowed by the visibility of the attribute or method acting against the attribute. If there is a SETTER method and it is public, maybe you can call it. Or if the attribute is public, you could simply change it directly, but it really depends on the class and what it is doing.

You could also check in your class where the instance attribute 'MD_ACTIVITY' is set. This can also happen at the level of the CONSTRUCTOR method. This would imply that there is no method available for changing this attribute.

If the attribute is not public or public yet 'read-only', then you probably have no programmatic means to change its value (except using the debugger).

Question 64: Switch the 'md_activity'

The attribute is set by the method 'FIND' from "CF_REBD_RENTAL_OBJECT". This method only works in activity 02 or 03. But I need to switch the 'md_activity' to 01 to go on with my program.

I also tried the same logic as you described:

```
data: go_specific_activity TYPE REF TO
CL_RECA_STORABLE.
go_specific_activity ?= EO_BUSOBJ.
go_specific_activity->IF_RECA_STORABLE~MD_ACTIVITY =
'01'.
```

But it's not allowed to change the 'read-only' attribute out of the class.

A: The logic of the factory class implies that the activity is set only once when the instance is created. The 'INIT_BUS_OBJECT' method should not be called twice, but this is up to you.

Question 65: Object 'go_rental_object'

Why is my object 'go_rental_object' found by the METHOD "cf_rebd_rental_object"=>find?

I only know this detail data and not all the other data like measures or characters.

A: RE-FX is basically OO-programming at its best.

Question: Should the rental object know details about its measurements?
Answer: No.

Question: Who Else?
Answer: The measurement mananger.

The rental object simply holds a reference to its measurement's manager which can be retrieved using method "GET_MEAS_MNGR".

For instance, the following questions and answers apply:

Question: Who knows the conditions for a rental object?
Answer: The condition manager (method GET_CONDITION_MNGR).

Question: Who knows the business partners of a rental object?
Answer: The partner manager (method GET_PARTNER_MNGR).

Question 66: Bound but empty

I tried your coding but I didn't get any measures from the manager. It's bound but empty, but my source-object has some.

Why did this happen? The result is the same with every manager I tried.

```
DATA:
        go_meas_mngr          TYPE REF TO
if_rebd_meas_mngr,
        go_RESUBM_RULE_MNGR TYPE REF TO
IF_RECA_RESUBM_RULE_MNGR,
        go_CHARACT_MNGR       type REF TO
IF_REBD_CHARACT_MNGR.


go_meas_mngr ?= go_rental_object->get_meas_mngr( ).
go_RESUBM_RULE_MNGR ?= go_rental_object-
>GET_RESUBM_RULE_MNGR( ).
go_CHARACT_MNGR ?= go_rental_object-
>GET_CHARACT_MNGR( ).
```

A: It is difficult to say where the problem is localized. I developed this sample report on our ECC 5.0 IDES system where I used an existing rental unit having several measurements.

I could imagine that it is a customizing problem. You could try and debug the instantiation of the measurement manager. Somewhere within its CONSTRUCTOR method there should be a (private or protected) method call which reads the measurements.

Perhaps you could try a more specific measurement manager like "CL_REBD_MEAS_MNGR_RO".

The managers only work with objects in change mode. In your code, you can change the mode to create.

Question 67: Problem with local class, static private attribute, and public method

Consider the following situation:

1) I have defined a LOCAL class airplane.
2) This class has a private static attribute "type table of ref to" airplane (array of airplanes).
3) A public method should return the private static table attribute

These are the problems encountered:

a) The table cannot be given an EXPORTING parameter in the method because 'TYPE TABLE OF' is not supported, and I get syntax errors. I also cannot define a dictionary table type because it is a local class.
b) The table cannot be given as a TABLES parameter in the method because TABLES is not supported in the OO context.
c) The table cannot be given as an EXPORTING parameter in the method defined as LIKE "myStaticAttribute" because my method is PUBLIC and my attribute is PRIVATE. ABAP syntax requires that all PUBLIC statements are defined before PRIVATE ones. Therefore, it cannot find the attribute to reference to with LIKE.

A: All relevant parts of the source code of a global class can be edited in the ABAP Editor: the "CLASS" statement for changing the class options, the three visiblity sections, and - of course - the method implementations.

Question 68: Calling a method

How can I call the method 'on_costing_component_to_outtab' which belongs to the class 'cl_im__gui_itemization_ck'?

The problem is that two of this method parameters '1_cl_cost_estimate' and '1_cl_costing_component' were referred to further classes.

I declared in the below faction and it worked fine when this method was on normal code. Inside this method, if some other class method is called it gave a dump saying that 'parameter '1_cl_cost_estimate' and '1_cl_costing_component' are passed null and could not recognize until runtime'.

How can I make this method work when there is one more class method called inside of this method?

If I am creating objects for '1_cl_cost_estimate' and '1_cl_costing_component', it stated "sub classes cannot be created".

```
Data: l_cl_exm_im_gui_itemization_ck TYPE REF TO
cl_im__gui_itemization_ck,
l_cl_cost_estimate TYPE REF TO cl_cost_estimate,
l_cl_costing_component TYPE REF TO
cl_costing_component.

create object: l_cl_exm_im_gui_itemization_ck.

CALL METHOD l_cl_exm_im_gui_itemization_ck-
>if_ex_gui_itemization_ck~on_costing_component_to_out
tab
EXPORTING
im_execution_service = l_ck_execution_service
im_cost_estimate = l_cl_cost_estimate "class
im_costing_component = l_cl_costing_component "class
im_gui_currency = l_ck_ewknz
CHANGING
ch_outtab_line = ws_ch_outtab_line.

-----------------------------------------------------
METHOD
if_ex_gui_itemization_ck~on_costing_component_to_outt
ab.
....
...
CALL METHOD im_cost_estimate->set_state
EXPORTING
im_calc_requested = ckc_yes.
```

```
ENDMETHOD.
--------------------------------------------------------
```

A: You cannot provide empty reference variables to the method, but you need to have instances of 'CL_COST_ESTIMATE' and/or 'CL_COSTING_COMPONENT'.

The 'CONSTRUCTOR' method of 'CL_COST_ESTIMATE' has an optional parameter "IM_QUANTITY" (of type CKBK_QUANTITY), and 'CL_COSTING_COMPONENT' has an optional parameter "IM_QUANTITY" (of type CKF_QUANTITY).

Based on your business scenario, you have to provide reasonable values for these importing parameters and create instances of both classes. These instances are then "fed" to method 'ON_COSTING_COMPONENT_TO_OUTTAB'.

Question 69: ABAP OO chain method call

Is it possible to use such bold statement in ABAP OO?

For example:

```
data: some_object type ref to dummy.

create object some_object.

some_object->get_another()-
>method_of_another_object().
```

I'm getting a reference in 'get_another' to another object. This object already exists.

A: I use frequently the interface 'IF_RECA_MESSAGE_LIST' as message handler for my classes. The interface is defined as instance attribute (e.g. MO_MSGLIST).

At the beginning of the CONSTRUCTOR method, I instantiate this interface:
me->mo_msglist = cf_reca_message_list=>create( ).

In order to collect SYST messages, I use the following method:
me->mo_msglist->add_symsg(id_detlevel = '1').

However, if your bolded statement implies that instance 'some_object' instantiates another object instance and simultaneously calls one of its methods, I do not think this is (yet) possible.

If I adjust my example to your logic, then the coding would look like this:

```
" some_object->get_another() ==>
cf_reca_message_list=>create( ) " returns instance
" method_of_another_object() ==> -add_symsg (of
returned instance)
  cf_reca_message_list=>create( )->add_symsg(
id_detlevel = '1' ).
```

In this case, I am convinced that is not possible.

I've checked it on two systems 6.4 and 7.0. On both application servers, it's not possible to use more than one method in one statement. Access to internal reference is only available via public reference fields.

Question 70: Strings in ABAP

What are strings?

What are the main uses of strings in ABAP?

Is there a real time scenario or example where we can use strings?

A: STRING is a bulit in data type and can be used to describe data objects of variable length. It is used to store text into variables in programs.

Example:

DATA: NAME TYPE STRING VALUE 'SANTOSH'.
Strings - Fields with Variable Length
The elementary data type STRING is similar to data type C and refers to a variable-length string. Accordingly, the elementary data type XSTRING is similar to data type X and refers to a variable-length byte sequence.

In contrast to a C or X field, the length of a string is not static but variable and adjusts itself to the current field content at runtime. Dynamic memory management is used internally. Strings can have any length.

The initial value of a string is an empty string with length 0. A structure containing a string is seen as deep. A deep structure cannot be used like a C field. Strings can be displayed in the ABAP Debugger and used in the ABAP Dictionary.

It is not yet possible to use strings in screens or database tables. However, strings can be stored in database tables as clusters using EXPORT and transferred using IMPORT.

The current release has not been possible to fully complete the implementation of strings. Especially the handling of blank characters at the end of a string has not been finalized for a number of ABAP statements.

For the highlighted argument positions of the following ABAP statements, blank characters at the end of strings are not taken into account. This may change in the next release. Therefore, strings with blank characters at the end should not be used in these positions.

ASSIGN f TO <fs> TYPEtype
ASSIGN TABLE FIELD (f)
ASSIGN (f) TO <fs>
ASSIGN LOCAL COPY OF MAIN TABLE FIELD (f) TO <fs>
ASSIGN COMPONENTname OF STRUCTURE struc TO <fs>
ASSIGN LOCAL COPY OF (f) TO <fs>
CALL SELECTION-SCREEN scr USING SELECTION-SETset
CLOSE DATASETdsn
CREATE OBJECT ref TYPE (class)
CREATE DATA dref TYPE (type)
DELETE FROM dbtab WHERE ...
(applies toall strings in the WHERE clause)
EDITOR-CALL FOR REPORTprog
EDITOR-CALL FOR itab TITLEtext
GENERATE DYNPRO ... IDid
GENERATE REPORTprog
GENERATE SUBROUTINE POOL itab NAMEname
IMPORT DYNPRO ... IDid
MESSAGE xnnn WITHf1 ...f4
MESSAGE ID id TYPEmtype NUMBERn
NEW-PAGE PRINT ON ... (applies toall additions)
OPEN DATASET dsn ...
... TYPEc
... MESSAGEm
... FILTERf
PERFORM (form)
... IN PROGRAM (prog)
SET PF-STATUSpfstat
... EXCLUDINGf
... OF PROGRAMprog
SET TITLEBARtitle
... OF PROGRAMprog
SET USER-COMMANDcmd
SUBMIT rep ... TO SAP-SPOOL ... (applies toall additions)
SUBMIT rep ... WITH FREE SELECTIONStexpr
TRANSFER f TOdsn
UPDATE dbtab WHERE ...
(applies toall strings in the WHERE clause)
WRITE ...
... CURRENCYw
... UNITu

Pre-defined Elementary ABAP Types with Variable Length

These pre-defined elementary data types are used to specify the types of individual fields whose lengths are not fixed until runtime. There are two pre-defined ABAP data types with variable length that are generically known as strings:

1. STRING for character strings
A string is a sequence of characters with variable length. A string can contain any number of alpha-numeric characters. The length of a string is the number of characters multiplied by the length required for the internal representation of a single character.

2. XSTRING for byte strings
A byte string is a hexa-decimal type with variable length. It can contain any number of bytes. The length of a byte string is the same as the number of bytes.

When you create a string as a data object, only a string header is created statically. This contains administrative information. The actual data objects are created and modified dynamically at runtime by operational statements.

The initial value of a string is the empty string with length 0. A structure that contains a string is handled like a deep structure. This means that there are no conversion rules for structures that contain strings.

Question 71: ABAP Mapping

What is the importance of ABAP Mapping and where is it applied?

A: This is a special case of XI Mapping in general. The other methods of mapping are xslt mapping/java mapping.graphical mapping and XSLT using ABAP. ABAP mapping (for that matter any mapping) would convert the source data which is in xml format, into target format (xml) as per rule.

Question 72: WE05 - hide the Tree

I am developing a new customized report with some additional fields for display by copying a standard WE05 code. I need to remove the Tree Display on the left hand side.

How can I accomplish this?

A: The tree is created in routine 'INIT_TREE' (screen '0100' -> module PBO -> routine INIT_TREE). At the end of the module PBO, you will see the following coding (6.20):

```
...
    if vh_tree is initial.
      perform init_tree.
    endif.
*   endif.
endmodule.
```

Question 73: CL_SALV_TREE

I'm using this class to build an ALV tree, besides I have functions (in a toolbar) to interact with the tree. Now, I found out that 'get_selected_nodes' etc. does not work with this kind of tree.

Will it work with 'cl_gui_column_tree'?

A: In using the CL_SALV_TREE classes, you have to think even more in an OO-based manner. Class CL_SALV_TREE does not have a method GET_SELECTED_NODES, but a method GET_SELECTIONS which returns a selection instance (CL_SALV_SELECTIONS_TREE). This class now has the required methods (e.g. GET_SELECTED_NODES, SET_SELECTED_ITEM, GET_SELECTED_COLUMNS).

Method GET_SELECTED_NODES returns a table with the selected nodes which were returned as node instances.

You have to call 'get_metadata' to get the data back from 'frontend'.

Question 74: Add 3rd child in simple tree

I have been able to add root, child1, and child2 using class CL_GUI_SIMPLE_TREE.
But when I tried to add child3, it gave the error 'Invalid access to database interface'.

Is there any constraint in using CL_GUI_SIMPLE_TREE?

A: Here's a piece of code:

```
        add 1 to childnr.
         concatenate 'child' childnr into childname.
         NODE-NODE_KEY =  childname.
         NODE-ISFOLDER = 'X'.
         NODE-EXPANDER = 'X'.
         ITEM-NODE_KEY = childname.
         move childname to vtab-childname.

         add 1 to dateinr.
         NODE-NODE_KEY =  dateinr.
         ITEM-NODE_KEY = node-node_key.
         move dateinr to vtab-childname.
       modify vtab from wa.
       APPEND ITEM TO ITEM_TABLE.
       APPEND NODE TO NODE_TABLE.
*Datum
       clear item.
       ITEM-NODE_KEY = NODE-NODE_KEY.
       ITEM-ITEM_NAME = '2'.
       ITEM-CLASS = CL_GUI_LIST_TREE=>ITEM_CLASS_TEXT.
       ITEM-LENGTH = 10.
       ITEM-USEBGCOLOR = 'X'.
       ITEM-TEXT = vtab-datum.
       APPEND ITEM TO ITEM_TABLE.
*Größe

       clear item.
       ITEM-NODE_KEY = NODE-NODE_KEY.
       ITEM-ITEM_NAME = '3'.
       ITEM-CLASS = CL_GUI_LIST_TREE=>ITEM_CLASS_TEXT.
       ITEM-LENGTH = 10.
       ITEM-USEBGCOLOR = 'X'.
       ITEM-TEXT = vtab-len.
       APPEND ITEM TO ITEM_TABLE.
*und los
```

```
CALL METHOD G_TREE->ADD_NODES_AND_ITEMS
  EXPORTING
    NODE_TABLE = NODE_TABLE
    ITEM_TABLE = ITEM_TABLE
    ITEM_TABLE_STRUCTURE_NAME = 'MTREEITM'
  EXCEPTIONS
    FAILED = 1
    CNTL_SYSTEM_ERROR = 3
    ERROR_IN_TABLES = 4
    DP_ERROR = 5
    TABLE_STRUCTURE_NAME_NOT_FOUND = 6.
IF SY-SUBRC <> 0.
  MESSAGE A000.
ENDIF.
```

There is no restriction regarding the number of child you can have. You have to check if you set the name and parents for child3 correctly.

Question 75: Error: Program " " not found

I created a dynamic table to display in ALV.

It gave me the following error:

```
MOVE i_fieldtab[] TO gt_fieldcat[].  " <-
incompatible structures
```

A: One change is:

```
CALL FUNCTION 'REUSE_ALV_FIELDCATALOG_MERGE'
EXPORTING
i_program_name = w_repid
i_structure_name = 'ZINVOICE'     " change to upper
case
i_inclname = w_repid
CHANGING
ct_fieldcat = i_fieldtab[].
```

The error cause lies here:

```
DATA: gt_fieldcat TYPE lvc_t_fcat.
i_fieldtab TYPE slis_t_fieldcat_alv WITH HEADER LINE,

MOVE i_fieldtab[] TO gt_fieldcat[].  " <-
incompatible structures
```

After the MOVE statement, the field catalog is completly messed up.

Question 76: Standard table into Z table

Is it possible to copy standard table (mara) into z table?

If it's possible, how can I do it?

A: It's possible to copy mara table. In se 11 screen, the copy push button is there. In there, you can specify your z table name and copy.

Question 77: Problem in selection from data base with RANGE-TABLE

I am facing a weird problem with range table in selection query. When I give an input to both 'ranges r_salesno,r_brandid' and the selection occurs, when I put black in one of those, it does not work.

I have passed 'Empty' table to range if there's no input in elements, even if it does not work.

What can be the reason why this is happening?

```
if  Stru_Cn_Selcrtr-ca_slsrl is not initial.
   wa_salesno-sign = 'I'.
   wa_salesno-option = 'EQ'.
   wa_salesno-LOW = Stru_Cn_Selcrtr-ca_slsrl.
   APPEND wa_salesno TO r_salesno.
   CLEAR : wa_salesno .
 else.
   wa_salesno-sign = 'I'.
   wa_salesno-option = 'EQ'.
   wa_salesno-LOW = space.
   APPEND wa_salesno TO r_salesno.
    CLEAR : wa_salesno .
 endif.


 if  Stru_Cn_Selcrtr-ca_brand is not initial.
   wa_brandid-sign = 'I'.
   wa_brandid-option = 'EQ'.
   wa_brandid-LOW = Stru_Cn_Selcrtr-ca_brand.
   APPEND  wa_brandid TO  r_brandid.
   CLEAR :  wa_brandid .
 else.
   wa_brandid-sign = 'I'.
   wa_brandid-option = 'EQ'.
    wa_brandid-LOW = space.

   APPEND wa_brandid  TO  r_brandid.
   CLEAR : wa_brandid   .
 endif.
```

```
*If any of these are given then select data
accordingly.
    <b>select * from ZNSLVWHDIMMD_LCL
             into corresponding fields of table
IT_VIEW
             WHERE SALESRLNO in  r_salesno
*             and   CREATEDBY in It_crtby_selopt
*            and   STARTDATE in It_validfrm_selopt
*             and   ENDDATE   in It_validto_selopt
*             and  STATUS     in It_status_selopt1
             and   BRANDID   in r_brandid.
*             and   MODELNO   in It_model_selopt.</b>
```

A: Your coding is problematic. I assume that field 'SALESRLNO' (of table ZNSLVWHDIMMD_LCL) probably means sales number (or sales order) and thus, must not be empty. If this is correct, then the first IF statement is probably wrong:

```
 if  Stru_Cn_Selcrtr-ca_slsrl is not initial.
    wa_salesno-sign = 'I'.
    wa_salesno-option = 'EQ'.
    wa_salesno-LOW = Stru_Cn_Selcrtr-ca_slsrl.
    APPEND wa_salesno TO r_salesno.
    CLEAR : wa_salesno .
  else.
    REFRESH: r_salesno.  " means: select all sales
numbers

" NOTE: If you fill the range like below this means
that only sales order
"            with no sales number (= ' ', space)
should be select.
" Thus, there will never be any sales order selected.
 *   wa_salesno-sign = 'I'.
 *   wa_salesno-option = 'EQ'.
 *   wa_salesno-LOW = space.
 *   APPEND wa_salesno TO r_salesno.
 *    CLEAR : wa_salesno .
  endif.
```

The same logic applies to the second IF statement. If you want to select all 'BRANDID' and none has been provided as selection criteria, then the code:

```
  if  Stru_Cn_Selcrtr-ca_brand is not initial.
    wa_brandid-sign = 'I'.
    wa_brandid-option = 'EQ'.
    wa_brandid-LOW = Stru_Cn_Selcrtr-ca_brand.
    APPEND  wa_brandid TO  r_brandid.
    CLEAR :  wa_brandid .
  else.
    REFRESH: r_brandid.  " means: select all BRANDID

*     wa_brandid-sign = 'I'.
*     wa_brandid-option = 'EQ'.
*      wa_brandid-LOW = space.
*
*     APPEND wa_brandid  TO  r_brandid.
*     CLEAR : wa_brandid  .
  endif.
```

Another suggestion is to use Dynamic Selection of data according to fields selected on selection screen.

Question 78: Kind of table

```
ATA: BEGIN OF line,
land(3) TYPE c,
name(10) TYPE c,
age TYPE i,
weight TYPE p DECIMALS 2,
END OF line.

DATA itab LIKE SORTED TABLE OF line
WITH NON-UNIQUE KEY land name age weight.
```

How can I know if the above example is a sorted, hashed, or standard table?

How do we know whether it should be hashed, sorted, or standard table of?

What criteria should we assign it to be sorted or hashed?

What would be the circumstance that I would declare so?

A: In the syntax, you declared internal table to be a sorted table of line.
Internal table is a sorted table.
DATA itab LIKE SORTED TABLE OF line -- sorted table

From the declaration of the internal table, we come to know whether it is standard, sorted or hashed table.

If nothing is declared, default will be the standard table.

The table type (and particularly the access method) that you will use depends on how the typical internal table operations will be most frequently executed.

Standard tables

This is the most appropriate type if you are going to address the individual table entries using the index. Index access is the quickest possible access. You should fill a standard table by appending lines (ABAP APPEND statement), and read, modify, and delete entries by specifying the index (INDEX option with the relevant ABAP command). The access time for a standard table increases in a linear relationship with the number of table entries. If you need key access, standard tables are particularly useful if you can fill and process the table in separate steps. For example, you could fill the table by appending entries, and then sort it. If you use the binary search option with key access, the response time is logarithmically proportional to the number of table entries.

Sorted tables

This is the most appropriate type if you need a table which is sorted as you fill it. You fill sorted tables using the INSERT statement. Entries are inserted according to the sort sequence defined through the table key. Any illegal entries are recognized as soon as you try to add them to the table. The response time for key access is logarithmically proportional to the number of table entries, since the system always uses a binary search. Sorted tables are particularly useful for partially sequential processing in a LOOP if you specify the beginning of the table key in the WHERE condition.

Hashed tables

This is the most appropriate type for any table where the main operation is key access. You cannot access a hashed table using its index. The response time for key access remains constant, regardless of the number of table entries. Like data base tables, hashed tables always have a unique key. Hashed tables are useful if you want to construct and use an internal table which resembles a database table, or for processing large amounts of data.
Depending on the access type used, you should use the appropriate table type for the definition in order to enable high performance access.

If you primarily key access - sorted /unique and non unique keys
Exclusively key access - hashed / unique keys
Primarily index access - standard /non unique keys

Question 79: Changing an internal table

Is it possible to change an internal table during run time? What are the scenarios where we might need this? Can you provide me an example program for this?

A: Yes, it is possible to change or modify an internal table at runtime.

Scenario:
1. Comparing with other table and need to be inserted.
2. Any mathematic operation to fill one more field from two other fields in same internal table.
3. To fill data which comes from the selection screen, screen data, or runtime data.

This is a simple code for modifying itab1 from itab2, where itab2 values is inserted into itab1-name1 is blank.

```
loop at itab1.
if itab1-name1 is initial.
read table itab2 with key kunnr = itab1-kunnr.
if sy-subrc = 0.
itab1-name1 = itab2-name1.
modify itab1 transporting name1.
endif.
endloop.
```

For further help, you can place the cursor on Modify and press F1. You will get help on how to write Modify statement with all possibilities.

For example, the above modify statement can also be written as:

```
MODIFY ITAB1 INDEX SY-TABIX.
```

If you also mean changing/appending/deleting the data in the internal during run time, you can do it in the debug mode.

Put a breakpoint on the append workarea to 'it_data', your code and execute.

Then, double click the internal table. You will see all the data in the internal table. Now, using the buttons i.e. append delete and some other buttons, you can insert or delete records from the internal table.

Question 80: Refresh cluster table "INDX"

How can I refresh the fields of the cluster table once after retreiving the data from it?

For example, in my scenario I have to write three programs where the output of the first program will be exported to the cluster table INDX using ID "program1", and in the second program this will be imported using ID "program1". The output of this second program will be exported to the cluster table INDX using ID "program2". This will be again imported in the third program using ID "program2". Now, once after importing the data from table INDX, I need to refresh the data from the table.

Can I have a code snippet or any standard example to get an idea?

A: In order to "refresh" the INDX table, use the DELETE statement as follows:

```
DELETE FROM { {MEMORY ID id}
            | {DATABASE      dbtab(ar) [CLIENT cl] ID
id}
            | {SHARED MEMORY dbtab(ar) [CLIENT cl] ID
id}
            | {SHARED BUFFER dbtab(ar) [CLIENT cl] ID
id} }.
```

You can also use EXPORT with a blank value for the ID "program1" and "program2".

Question 81: Sorted table of ref to if_ixml_element

I would like to define an internal table of ref to if_ixml_element using a non-linear number key (read: there are gaps in the key, its not 1,2,3,4 its 1,4,5,6 for example).

I cannot seem to get the syntax down correctly.

I have tried the statement below and received error message "no component exists with type I".

```
DATA M_ROW_ELEMENTS type SORTED TABLE OF ref to
IF_IXML_ELEMENT WITH UNIQUE KEY I.
```

I tried generic declaration as follows and received error message "Key specification is incomplete".

```
DATA M_ROW_ELEMENTS type SORTED TABLE OF ref to
IF_IXML_ELEMENT .
```

Also:

```
DATA M_ROW_ELEMENTS type SORTED TABLE OF ref to
IF_IXML_ELEMENT WITH UNIQUE KEY idx.
```

What am I doing wrong?

A: Create a class and implement your Interface, and also declare a table as attribute of class.

Now, you can create an object of class in which you will have your internal table.

If you have an itab containing instances of classes, then you can sort these instances by any public attribute of the class as follows:

```
*&---------------------------------------------------------*
*& Report  ZUS_SDN_SORTED_ITAB_REFERENCE
*&
*&---------------------------------------------------------*
*&
*&
*&---------------------------------------------------------*
```

```
REPORT  zus_sdn_sorted_itab_reference.

DATA:
  go_ixml    TYPE REF TO cl_ixml,
  gt_itab    TYPE TABLE OF REF TO cl_ixml.



START-OF-SELECTION.

  " NOTE: class CL_IXML has a public attribute
M_POINTEE.
  "       Sorting of the itab containing references
of the class
  "       by this public attribute is possible:

  SORT gt_itab BY table_line->m_pointee.    " for
BINARY SEARCH


  READ TABLE gt_itab INTO go_ixml
       WITH KEY table_line->m_pointee = '<key value>'
       BINARY SEARCH.


END-OF-SELECTION.
```

Just an addendum to the obviously useful answers above...
Since IF_IXML_ELEMENT does not have any public attributes, why don't you try adding the number field(your index) as a field in your Itab?

```
DATA: BEGIN OF rline,
          number TYPE i,
          rif TYPE REF TO IF_IXML_ELEMENT,
          END OF rline,
          rtab LIKE SORTED TABLE OF rline WITH UNIQUE
KEY number.
```

Then whenever you insert a line to the Itab, assign it a unique index number.

For example, if you have an object reference in r_obj:

```
rline-number = 1.
"Keep incrementing number or use your own specific
logic
rline-rif = r_obj.

INSERT rline TO TABLE rtab.
```

Whenever you wish to retrieve your reference:

```
READ TABLE rtab INTO rline
        WITH TABLE KEY number = currnum.
"currnum = value of index you're looking for";
```

Question 82: Internal table as an OO way of handling data in a report/program

Is the internal table an OO compliant way of handling data in a report/program?

Or there is any alternative full-fledged OO way for replacing an internal table?

A: Internal tables are fully "OO-compliant". However, they must not have header lines. In order to use internal tables as parameters in public methods, you have to use globally accessible table types (that have been defined in the DDIC, either directly as table types or as table type definition within type-pools). Using type-pool definitions, you have to declare them on the Properties tabstrip (SE24).

If you declare an internal table within the OO context, say within a method, you can not declare it using the OCCURS keyword either. You must declare using TYPE TABLE OF, and then declare an explicit work area .

```
data: imara type table of mara.
data: xmara like line of imara.
```

Question 83: User exit not triggered

We are in ECC6.0. I need to change the PO vendor confirmations (EKES) in ME22n transaction. I have written a code in 'EXIT_SAPMM06E_013' transaction. The code is not triggering. I had put Break-point in the code. It is not stopping while saving the ME22N transaction.

Is there any special configuration required to activate this 'User exit'?

A: Check if you have created a project (transaction CMOD) and assigned the component of enhancement MM06E005. If you have created, please ensure that you have activated the component enhancement MM06E005 and also the project as well.

Question 84: GUI_DOWNLOAD inside a BSP METHOD

I have a BSP application and in the application class, I have a method named 'TXT_FACTURA'.

Inside of it, I need to save a text file to local machine, so I tried to use the FM:

GUI_DOWNLOAD
or
WS_DOWNLOAD

But when the BSP arrives to execute this FM, a HTTP 500 error raised me.
Why did this happen?

I tested this FM with the same data in a separated report, and all went fine.

A: You can not use these front-end (sapgui) dependent function modules within a BSP. BSP runs in the browser, so there is no SAPgui. These function modules use code within the SAPgui itself to complete their task.

Question 85: Field catalogs with an example

Which is more efficient, defining the field catalog manually or automatically?

What is field catalog? What should I know about it?

A: Manual code creation will generally by more efficient than code written by a machine.

Question 86: Use of link method in 'cl_gui_custom_container'

What is the use of link method in custom container?

How can I get the documents against the methods of the classes?

A: Instead of connecting a container hard-wired to a screen using a custom container as screen element, you can dynamically link a container to a screen. The advantage is that you can easily re-link this container to another screen which is not possible in the previous case.

The following sample report shows how a docking container is dynamically linked to screen '0100'.

Sample report ZUS_SDN_TWO_ALV_GRIDS

In order to test the re-linking, simply create a second screen (e.g. '0200') and add coding in the PAI module (USER_COMMAND_0100), the following coding:

```
* Link the docking container to the second screen

IF ( gd_okcode = 'ENTER' ).

  CALL METHOD go_docking->link
    EXPORTING
      repid                            = syst-repid
      dynnr                            = '0200'
*       CONTAINER                       =
    EXCEPTIONS
      OTHERS                           = 4.
  IF sy-subrc <> 0.
*   MESSAGE ID SY-MSGID TYPE SY-MSGTY NUMBER SY-MSGNO
*              WITH SY-MSGV1 SY-MSGV2 SY-MSGV3 SY-
MSGV4.
  ENDIF.

ENDIF.
```

The docking container is now attached to the second screen.

Crucial point: Linking containers instead of using hard-wired ones enhances re-usability.

You can also check the demo program "RSDEMO_CUSTOM_CONTROL".

Question 87: Issue with CL_BCS

I am pasting a part of the code which I am working on now. This is related to sending an e-mail using class CL_BCS. I am trying to send an e-mail with more than 50 characters in it.

I know that the problem is with the bolded part. When I went into the debugger mode, I see that it compares the subject line which is passed on to the i_subject.

How can I link the object document with the method 'set_message_subject'?

Try:
```
* -------- create persistent send request ----------
-------------
send_request = cl_bcs=>create_persistent( ).


* -------- create and set document with attachment --
-------------
* create document from internal table with text
document = cl_document_bcs=>create_document(
i_type = 'RAW'
i_text = text
i_length = '12'
i_subject = i_subject ).


*subject line more than 50 chars
data: t_sub type string.
t_sub = 'This is too ridiculous but lets just test
this whether this will work out for more than 50
chars'.

CALL METHOD send_request->set_message_subject
EXPORTING
ip_subject = t_sub.


*changing the content of the attachment
binary_content[] = l_iobjbin[].

*change the name of the PDF attachment
concatenate 'Build ID' s_buildid_i 'Rev'
v_buildid_rev
into i_att_sub separated by space.

* add attachment to document
CALL METHOD document->add_attachment
EXPORTING i_attachment_type = 'PDF'
i_attachment_subject = i_att_sub
i_att_content_hex = binary_content.
```

```
* add document to send request
CALL METHOD send_request->set_document( document ).
```

A: Refer program BCS_EXAMPLE*. You need to change the configuration settings in SCOT.

Set SMTP node to 'node in use'. Go to 'Internet settings' and then say '*' in the address area.

Question 88: In need of a push button event handler for a cl_gui_custom_container

I have two cl_gui_custom_containers. Container1 has a double click event receiver that when fired, it displays a long text using the 'READ_TEXT' function module displaying in Container2. I am trying to add a push button to Container2, to print contents of the screen but not the Container1 ALV.

How can I do this?

A: You cannot add a push button to a container. Instead, you could add an additional container with a toolbar having the required buttons.

However, I would recommend to define a simple GUI-status having a push button "PRINT". When the user pushes this button, you simply call in PAI of the dynpro function module PRINT_TEXT. This function module is within the same function group as READ_TEXT.
For details about fm PRINT_TEXT, refer to its documentation.

Question 89: BAPI_MATERIAL_SAVEDATA cost currency issue

I'm using 'BAPI_MATERIAL_SAVEDATA' to create new materials. When entering the 'BAPI_MBEW-STD_PRICE' value, it returns the following error: "37CURRENCY initial v., currency amount 500.00 in STD_PRICE was transferred without a currency".

The problem is that I cannot find anywhere in this BAPI where I can enter the currency equivalent to USD. What can be the answer for this?

The currency we use is always in USD. I am not getting any other values outside of USD. I cannot find where to tell this BAPI that the currency is USD. There is no need for currency translation.

I tried PRICE_CTRL = 'V' and PRICE_UNIT = '1', but I received the same error message. I'm trying everything that makes sense to me at this end. I have been examining existing materials, as well to find clues, but nothing so far.

A: Before passing the value 'BAPI_MBEW-STD_PRICE', convert into local currency or foreign currency and check the results.

Also check if you are not including the plant information. It would appear that the currency (table T001) is pulled in by the BAPI based on plant.

Question 90: CX_SHM_EXTERNAL_REFERENCE exc. when passing Class instance to Shared memory

When setting-up writing to a shared memory (using the SHMA and SHMM transactions), we get an exception mentioning CX_SHM_EXTERNAL_REFERENCE.

This problem was raised because we were trying to move an instantiated class from the calling development to the Shared memory class. Therefore, this exception was raised. The SAP standard documentation tells me:

"There are still references from the current area instance version to a different area instance of the shared objects memory, or to the internal session."

How can we work around this problem? I really want to pass the instantiated class to the Shared memory.

A: You can try to avoid references to other objects inside the code of the shared class. i.e. no CREATE OBJECT inside constructor or methods of the shared class.

Question 91: Moving a BOR ".bmp" attachment (objtyp message) to a Picture Control

```
Using BAPI_REL_GETRELATIONS and the usual SWC macros,
I am able to:

1) Find the "objectid" of a BOR object of type
"MESSAGE" that contains a ".bmp" attachment to a PM
notification;

2) Create an instance of this object in background.

But now that I have an instance of the object which
holds the actual ".bmp", what do I have to do to
provide this ".bmp" to a picture control on a screen
?

I know I can display the ".bmp" in a variety of ways,
e.g. using the 'display_attachment' method of
"CL_GOS_DOCUMENT_SERVICE".

How do I give a picture control addressability to a
".bmp" held in the BOR as an object?
```

A: For a given PM notification, I attached a '.bmp' file via GOS. Using your logic, I can retrieve the link to the graphic. However, there is a little error within my logic because I do not use the object data of the graphic file but of the PM notification in order to display the graphic.

Apparently, my solution works properly if there is a single '.bmp' file attached to the PM notification.

Question 92: CL_GUI_TOOLBAR button doesn't fire from custom subscreen

I have a subscreen on a custom tab in IW22.

This subscreen is prepared by the "ZXQQMU07" module included by exit EXIT_SAPMIWO0_008 in XQQM.

In the ZXQQMU07 module, I have created a toolbar, added a button to this toolbar, and created an event receiver which is defined in my ZXQQMC01 module included from ZXQQMZZZ. I've also remembered to set the handler for the event.

The toolbar shows fine on the subscreen with the button on it.

But when I clicked the button, nothing happens.

What is wrong? I just don't see it.

A: Set up an event and then register the event.

General Information FAQ

Question 93: Update was terminated in VF02

I have added two segments to the Invoice idoc INVOIC02. In the user exit EXIT_SAPLVEDF_002, inside Include ZXEDFU02, I have another include
by name include yxedfu02_us.

Inside this, I have added the code to populate the two added segments for E1EDK01.

Now, I am facing a problem in creating or changing a billing document in VF01/VF02.
I am entering data for output. I navigated to HEADER- OUTPUT in vf02. There, I am giving YU10 (for EDI output). The first problem is this YU10 is displayed with yellow status icon. Secondly, when I save, come out, and go into vf02 again for the same billing document, it shows "Update was terminated".

I went to SM13 and found the error.

In the include where I have added the code, they have used a table INT_EDIDD.
It shows an error while I check the include. It says "INT_EDIDD does not exist as table or data".

But if I double click on 'INT_EDIDD', it navigates to the user exit function module 'EXIT_SAPLVEDF_002' table declaration INT_EDIDD structure EDIDD.

Where did it go wrong?

A: The table INT_EDIDD will only be recognized within the outer include zxedfu02.
To access this from a sub-routine in another include, you must pass it to the sub-routine using the table's statement.

Question 94: Type problems

I'm trying to send emails via 'cl_bcs'. It's working great when I define the receivers on my own with:

```
    recipient =
cl_cam_address_bcs=>create_internet_address(
                    'mail@adress.com' ).

    CALL METHOD send_request->add_recipient
      EXPORTING
        i_recipient   = recipient
        i_express     = 'X'.
```

But when I'm using a list of email addresses from an internal table, I get the error "it_receivers-email is not type compatible to formal parameter i_address_string" (translated from german error text). "it_receivers-email" is declared as string.

Why isn't this working?

```
loop at it_receivers.
       recipient =
cl_cam_address_bcs=>create_internet_address(
                    it_receivers-email ).
       ...
endloop.
```

A: You might want to use a work area instead.

```
data: wa_receivers like line of it_receivers.

loop at it_receivers into wa_receivers.
       recipient =
cl_cam_address_bcs=>create_internet_address(
                    wa_receivers-email ).
       ...
endloop.
```

You should try to type your field like ADR6-SMTP_ADDR instead of string.

Question 95: Spool Generation problem

What is the problem in the spool generation of the following scenario?

I have two reports: ZF003 and ZF005. ZF003 contains the ALV grid which actually outputs the list. If I run this in background, the spool is being generated because it makes use of ALV grid. We had a requirement to code some additional functionality in ZF005 and made use of ZF003 in the program ZF005. ZF005 displays the ALV output when it is running in foreground. But it is not generating the spool when run in the background.

What went wrong?

A: Check ZF003 if it is also ALV or a simple list using write statements. Make sure there are no write statements when using ALV.

Also check if that program handles any Upload or Download from PC.

Make sure you check the status of the job and if it is successful.

You can also try to code in ZF005 using ALV once again to generate the spool in background.

Question 96: Workflow

While creating the task, when I tried to save the task it asked for a prefix number.

How can I give the prefix number and save it?

A: Usually, this is done on the basis of the development system and it requires authorization access. But you could try the following on the system you're using:

1. Tcode SWU3.

2. Maintain Definition Environment->Maintain Prefix Numbers.

3. Click on execute or F8.

It's similar to creating number ranges.

Question 97: Modularization Techniques Tutorial

Where can I find a Modularization Techiques Tutorial?

I need it for both Local Modularization and Include Program.

A: All ABAP programs are modular in structure and made up of processing blocks (see Structure of ABAP Programs). There are two kinds of processing blocks, those that are called from outside a program by the ABAP runtime system, and those that can be called by ABAP statements in ABAP programs.

These are the processing blocks that are called using the ABAP runtime system:

Event blocks
Dialog modules
Processing blocks that are called from ABAP programs:

Subroutines
Function modules
Methods
The processing blocks that you call from ABAP programs are called procedures.

As well as modularization in processing blocks, ABAP allows you to modularize source code by placing ABAP statements either in local macros or global include programs.

This section of the documentation describes both modularizations in source code modules and in procedures. This kind of modularization makes ABAP programs easier to read and maintain, as well as avoiding redundancy, increasing the reusability of source code, and encapsulating data.

Splitting up ABAP programs into event blocks and dialog modules is designed to help the general flow of the programs.

You can also check transaction ABAPDOCU in SAP for sample programs.

Question 98: Sub-routine

I think there's a mistake in my sub-routine.

Code:

```
FORM check_loesch CHANGING p_ch_meld TYPE gts_meld.

DATA: ls_objnr TYPE qmel-objnr,
ls_stat TYPE jest-stat.

CONCATENATE 'QM' p_ch_meld-qmnum INTO ls_objnr.

SELECT SINGLE stat FROM jest
INTO ls_stat
WHERE objnr = ls_objnr
AND stat = 'I0076' "LÖVM
AND inact = space.
IF sy-subrc = 0.
p_ch_meld-status = gc_status-deleted.
ENDIF.
```

What's wrong with my code?

A: Perhaps the notification number is missing leading zeros.

Please note that you must not use the coding like this:

```
CONCATENATE 'QM' p_ch_meld-qmnum INTO ls_objnr.
```

It's because this is a quick-and-dirty programming (and error-prone as well).

Question 99: Problem in PF status

I have created a PF status and added a push button on the 'Application' toolbar. I passed this PF status in the function module. 'REUSE_ALV_LIST_DISPLAY'.

When the report is executed, only the push button appears on the screen. All the default Application tool bar items and menu items disappear.

How can I handle this situation?

A: You need to copy the PF status, the standard ALV report 'SAPLSLVC_FULLSCREEN', and status STATUS. Then, make the modification like adding a button.

Another suggestion is to copy the standard PF status 'STANDARD', and then add your button in that copied PF status. Then pass that PF status. You will see the default buttons too.

You can also check-out the standard program "bcalv_grid_05".

Question 100: Adding new field to Me21n transaction

I need to add a new field, say cost center in Me21n transaction in 'Account Assignment' tab of ITEM. I should be able to save it in the EKPO table.

What is the process or code?

A: It is different in 4.6C or ECC5/6. The easiest is via BADI in ECC or user exit in 4.6C.

Go into SPRO and open the MM->PO node. You will find there the documentation on how to do it. You can also go to SE19 and open the SAP components under MM.

You can also try the following:

1) Go to SMOD transaction.
2) Enter the enhancement name "MM06E005".
3) Click on the components radion button in display mode.
4) Now, you will find the screen exits as:

SAPMM06E 0111 CUSTSCR1 SAPLXM06 0111 Subscreen: PO item

5) Go to that particular code (se51->Program and screen number "SAPMM06E 0111").
6) Create a new sub-screen for adding the required field.

Question 101: Make text edit visible/invisible

In PBO, I created a text edit object of 'class cl_gui_textedit' as follows:

```
* Check Result textedit
    CREATE OBJECT chk_rslt
           EXPORTING parent = container_middle.
    CALL METHOD chk_rslt->SET_TOOLBAR_MODE
        EXPORTING TOOLBAR_MODE = 0.
    CALL METHOD chk_rslt->SET_STATUSBAR_MODE
        EXPORTING statusbar_MODE = 0.
```

I would like this object to be invisible at this point.

Later at some point depending on some other events, I want to make this text edit object visible.

I was looking at the methods and properties of 'class cl_gui_textedit' but couldn't find anything suitable. I believe there is something in that class which can be used to accomplish my task.

What can be the solution for this?

A: You can use the inherited method SET_VISIBLE. Set it to "X" when you want it to be visible, and space when not.

Question 102: Use of sy-dynnr and sy-prog

What is the use of sy-dynnr and sy-prog in the selection screen based programs?

A: sy-dynnr - to get the current screen and store the current screen number.
sy-cprog - to get main program. It stores the calling program when in a procedure (FM or routine). If a procedure called externally calls another external procedure, sy-cprog contains the name of the framework program, and is not set to the name of the framework program of the subsequent calling program.

Question 103: Send mail step of workflow

Is it possible to create a new task for the send mail step of the workflow, instead of using the standard task TS45308726-send mail?

A: Yes it is very much possible.

All you have to do is to create a method in a class that will send the desired e-mail. Inside this method, you can call any send e-mail function module (for example, SO_SEND_OBJECT or SO_OBJECT_SEND. I'm not sure of the order, but you should be able to find it). After that, generate a task that calls this method (using transaction PFTC).

After you finish, you can insert this newly created task into your workflow template.

Question 104: Change public instance attribute

I have to change a value vom a structure. It's a public instance attribute from the 'superclass'.

How can I change it?

This is the coding:

```
go_busobj_created-ms_detail-nr = '1020'.
```

It shows an error that 'go_busobj_created' is an object reference and doesn't own a component "ms_detail-snunr". But in debugging, I can navigate with double click into 'ms_detail' and I can change manually the value.

The other way I tried is using the method from a super class that my object (go_busobj_created) inherits during runtime. But I don't know how to call it.

```
call METHOD CL_SUPERCLASS=>('SET_NR')
```

or

```
call METHOD ('IF_SUPERCLASS~SET_NR')
```

I can call static or dynamic everytime it dumps.

I defined it like this:

```
DATA go_busobj_created TYPE REF TO IF_BUS_OBJECT.
```

In this IF, the Object doesn't know the methods or the attribute. It's known only during program runtime.

The "go_busobj_created" is created by another method I called (create obj by template).

Is it relevant?

A: If it's an instance attribute, first you have to create an object reference to your class. Then you can modify the attribute of that instance.

```
data: gro_something type ref to cl_myclass.
...
create object gro_something.
...
gro_something-ms_detail-nr = '1020'.
```

Based on my knowledge from RE-FX, I assume that "GO_BUSOBJ" is a very generic object reference. Thus, in order to access the instance attribute 'MS_DETAIL', you have to do a narrowing cast:

```
DATA:
  go_busobj        TYPE REF TO <generic class>,
  go_specific       TYPE REF TO <specific class which
is a subclass of generic class>.

  go_specific ?= go_busobj.  " narrowing cast
  go_specific_created->ms_detail-nr = '1020'.
```

```
For example, the BDT function modules in RE-FX pass
most (if not all) object references as TYPE REF TO
cl_reca_storable. The actual object may be a contract
(CL_RECN_CONTRACT), a building (CL_REBD_BUILDING), or
some other RE object.
```

Question 105: Docking container and SAP standard transaction

In one screen, I have a tree control container and a docking container. With the tree control container, everything is perfect. If the user clicks on a node on the tree in the docking container, it should shown a SAP standard transaction (QA03) with the corresponding data.

I have not found a possibility to show QA03 or QM03 in a docking container. I also tried it in a splitter container, but I do not know how.

How can I do this?

A: There is a simple answer to your question: it is not possible.

A container can only hold other containers or controls. Do not be fooled by the ABAP workbench where we apparently can switch between different transactions (e.g. display a class [SE24], show method coding [SE80], double-click on a DDIC structure [SE11]). The ABAP workbench simply changes the control to be displayed but NOT the transaction (remains always the same).

Question 106: Description of matnr (maktx)

There is a method that selects 'maktx' for each 'sy-langu', what is it?

A: You can try the following to select 'maktx' from the 'makt table': Select maktx from makt into table it_makt for all entries in it_mara where matnr = it_mara-matnr.

```
  if sy-subrc = 0.

 endif.
```

In MAKt, the material text is maintained for multiple languages. Normally, we insert 'sy-langu' to restirct system to return material test in user logon language.
Example:

select single maktx into <some_variable>
from makt where matnr = <some_material_variable>
and spras = sy-langu.

However if you want it for all languages, just omit the 'where' clause comparing language (and spras = sy-langu) and it will return the material texts in all the languages where it is maintained. like

select maktx into <some_variable>
from makt where matnr = <some_material_variable>
*** > <some_variable> will contain material text. since language (spras) is
***> not mentioned, it will run for all languages maintained in MAKT
endselect.

If it's about a function module, try 'READ_TEXT'. It's a function module used for reading long texts, so I'm not sure if it will work. It also has a language field to separate out between languages.
If the company is located in different countries then they will have different languages, so we need to maintain materials in different languages.

* Single material description

```
select single maktx from makt into makt-maktx
where matnr = '9999'
spras = 'EN'.
```

The above query (MAKT is the material text table) gets the data from 'makt table' using matnr value and spras (langauge).

Here, maktx is material description.

* See if you want to get all the language, then do not use select single.

```
select maktx from makt into table i_makt
where matnr = '9999'.
```

In here, 'i_makt' is the internal table. It will get the material number with different languages.

Question 107: "is bound"

I would like to know the meaning of the phrase 'is bound', as in: IF htmlb_event IS BOUND AND htmlb_event->name = 'button'.

A: With this statement, you check whether a reference variable holds indeed an instance of a class. For example, when we have a dynpro with a container where you display an ALV grid, you should instantiate the controls (container and ALV grid) only once.

```
DATA:
  go_container     TYPE REF TO
cl_gui_custom_container,
  go_grid               TYPE REF TO cl_gui_alv_grid.

MODULE init_controls OUTPUT.

  IF ( go_container IS NOT BOUND ).
    CREATE OBJECT go_containe
       ...

    IF ( go_container IS BOUND ).
      CREATE OBJECT go_grid
        EXPORTING
          parent = go_container
          ...
    ENDIF.

  ELSE.  " ( go_container IS BOUND ).

  ENDIF.

ENDMODULE.
```

Question 108: SPAU without modification assistant

I'm on an upgrade project, "In SPAU tcode > without modification assistant> programs". When I'm going for version management, it's displaying some 10 modified versions of the program. From those versions, which do I have to keep in my new version?

Second, which of these versions do I have to choose?

Third, what about this modified version which is displayed on the top?

A: The versions shown are based on the changes done. Let's say a particular object went under change 10 times, so you are getting that many versions. The latest version is always on the top.

As the latest version is 00012, so it should be there in the system. But check if you want some changes from version 11 also.

The easiest way to find the transaction related to user exits is using the 'where used list'.

Just do a 'where used list' and you will find the program name (mostly include). Using that, you can find the main program and the related transaction.

Keep the active version as it is the most recent. Just from the comparision, you are able to find out what are those changes. Check if they are upgrade related or they are customer specific.

Question 109: Grid and List display

What is the difference between "REUSE_ALV_LIST_DISPALY" and "REUSE_ALV_GRID_DISPALY"?

A: For all practical purposes, they are the same.

The following are some differences:

a) From ABAP coding point of view, ALV list is done with Function modules.
ALV grids can also be done with FM, but can also be done using OO concepts.

b) ALV grid (using OO concept) requires designing the screen layout.
Hence, in one screen we can show more, but then only one ALV grid (we cannot show more than
one ALV list in one screen).

c) ALV grid uses ActiveX controls present on the Presentation Server.
Hence, it consumes more Memory on the presentation server.

d) ALV LIST is Display Only. Whereas, ALV Grid can be made EDITABLE for entry purposes.

e) In ALV grid, these options are possible but not in ALV list:

- without horizontal lines
- without vertical lines
- without cell merging during sorts
- display total lines above the entries

ALV LIST can be coded using only FMs.
ALV GRID can be coded using FMs and object oriented concepts.

ALV LIST can be displayed in hierarchy.
ALV GRID cannot be displayed in hierarchy.

In ALV list, we can't display logo in the screen, but we can display logo in ALV report using ALV grid.

In ALV list, we can display footer messages, but we can't in ALV grid.

We can also display data in stripped manner using ALV grid.

Question 110: Make an input field inactive

I'm writing a report to delete a document of a Business Partner. I have an input template with two Input fields (BP and Document) and two radio buttons (display and delete).

I want to de-activate the document input field when the display button is checked. It means it should not be possible to enter any data in the document field when the display button is checked.

I tried with at screen:

```
if pa_dis = 'X'.
if screen-name = 'PA_PROG'.
screen-active = 0.
screen-invisible = 1.
endif.
```

but it didn't help.

How can I do this?

A: You can do this in two ways

1. Delete the code entirely.
2. Comment out the code.

Best programming practice would dictate that you comment out the code for later reference.

Question 111: Overloading & overriding

What is the difference between overloading and overriding?

A: In overloading, there is a relationship between methods available in the same class. Whereas in overriding, there is a relationship between a superclass method and a subclass method.

Overloading does not block inheritance from the superclass, whereas overriding blocks inheritance from the superclass.

In overloading, separate methods share the same name. In overriding, subclass method replaces the superclass.

Overloading must have different method signatures, while overriding must have the same signature.

```
CLASS zl_lcl_vehicle DEFINITION.

PUBLIC SECTION.
* Signature of method
METHODS: set_make
IMPORTING value(im_make) TYPE string " Pass by value
im_model TYPE string," Pass by reference

ENDCLASS. "zl_lcl_vehicle DEFINITION

CLASS zl_lcl_vehicle IMPLEMENTATION.
* Implementation of method.
METHOD set_make.

IF im_make IS NOT INITIAL
AND im_model IS NOT INITIAL.
gv_make = im_make.
gv_model = im_model.
ENDIF.

ENDMETHOD. "set_make
ENDCLASS. "zl_lcl_vehicle
```

Another definition is Overloading means changing signature as well as implementation of a method.

Overriding is changing only implementation of method with signature unchanged.
From ABAP perspective, only the CONSTRUCTOR method can be overloaded in a subclass. I.e. both the signature and

implementation can be adapted in subclass.

Any other method can't be overloaded. It can only be re-defined/overridden. I.e. implementation changed with signature unchanged.

Question 112: Workbench request

I need a help regrading requests which we created at the beginning of any object.
I created a different request for driver program and a script.
Now, I want to merge both requests.

Is it possible whether it is released or not?

A: The owner of the request can move the tasks from one request to the other. Right click on 'task' and see the options you get. So you can move all the tasks of one request to the other, provided the request is not released.

Question 113: Conditional statements

What are the differences between exit, check, continue, and stop?

A: EXIT= it gets you out of the current processing block. Inside a loop, it would get you out of the loop (even if it is inside some processing block inside the loop). In start-of-selection event, it gets you out of the program.

CHECK= it would get you out of the current processing block if the condition is met.

CONTINUE= goes to the next loop pass.

STOP= comes out of the start-of-selection event and goes to the first statement of end-of-selection.

This is taken from F1 help:

Terminating Loops

ABAP contains termination statements that allow you to terminate a loop prematurely. There are two categories of termination statement - those that only apply to the loop, and those that apply to the entire processing block in which the loop occurs. The STOPand REJECT statements belong to the latter group (see Exiting Eventblocks).

The termination statements that apply only to the loop in which they occur are CONTINUE, CHECKand EXIT. You can only use the CONTINUE statement in a loop. CHECK and EXIT, on the other hand, are context-sensitive. Within a loop, they only apply to the execution of the loop itself. Outside of a loop, they terminate the entire processing block in which they occur (subroutine, dialog module, event block, and so on).

CONTINUE, CHECK and EXITcan be used in all four loop types in ABAP (DO, WHILE, LOOP and SELECT).

Terminating a Loop Pass Unconditionally
To terminate a single loop pass immediately and unconditionally, use the CONTINUE statement in the statement block of the loop.

CONTINUE.

After the statement, the system ignores any remaining statements in the current statement block, and starts the next loop pass.

```
DO 4 TIMES.
IF sy-index = 2.
CONTINUE.
ENDIF.
WRITE sy-index.
ENDDO.
```

The list output is:

1 3 4

The second loop pass is terminated without the WRITE statement being processed.

Terminating a Loop Pass Conditionally
To terminate a single loop pass conditionally, use the CHECK condition statement in the statement block of the loop.

CHECK condition.

If the condition is not true, any remaining statements in the current statement block after the CHECK statement are ignored, and the next loop pass starts. condition can be any logical expression.

```
DO 4 TIMES.
CHECK sy-index BETWEEN 2 and 3.
WRITE sy-index.
ENDDO.
```

The list output is:

2 3

The first and fourth loop passes are terminated without the WRITE statement being processed, because sy-index is not between 2 and 3.

Exiting a Loop

To terminate an entire loop immediately and unconditionally, use the EXIT statement in the statement block of the loop.

EXIT.

After this statement, the loop is terminated, and processing resumes after the closing statement of the loop structure (ENDDO, ENDWHILE, ENDLOOP, ENDSELECT). In nested loops, only the current loop is terminated.

```
DO 4 TIMES.
IF sy-index = 3.
EXIT.
ENDIF.
WRITE sy-index.
ENDDO.
```

The list output is:

1 2

In the third loop pass, the loop is terminated before the WRITE statement is processed.

Within a loop structure:

EXIT Within a loop structure: Terminates loop processing (DO, WHILE, LOOP, SELECT).
Within sub-routines and other modularization units (but not in a loop structure):
Leaves the sub-routine or modularization unit (FORM, MODULE, FUNCTION, TOP-OF-PAGE, END-OF-PAGE).
Outside loop structures and modularization units (report processing):
Terminates report processing and triggers list display.

CONTINUE Within loop structures, terminates the current loop pass, returns the processing to the beginning of the loop and starts the next loop pass, if there is one.

CHECK if condition is true, the processing continues with the next statement else work like CONTINUE.

STOP This statement terminates a processing block in an executable program. (exit from an INITIALIZATION, AT SELECTION-SCREEN, START-OF-SELECTION, and GET events and go to END-OF-SELECTION) better use EXIT.

Question 114: Link the container and screen

I have splitted the screeno to 3 containers. The first one is for pic, the second is for tree, and the last one for display guid. It is all ok like the SAP program 'DEMO_ABAP_OBJECTS_SPLIT_SCREEN'.

Now I want a container to display a screen/subscreen which I have created. How can I do it?

select_s TYPE REF TO
cl_gui_custom_container/cl_gui_custom_container
CREATE OBJECT select_s
EXPORTING
parent = container_top " the splited container
container_name = 'Container_1'
repid = sy-repid
dynnr = '0200'. " the created screen

A: Instead of splitting your screen into three containers, I would use a single container on the screen and place a splitted container into this screen container.

In the sample report, I have linked the docking container (holding a splitter container for three ALV lists) to the entire screen:

```
* Link the docking container to the target dynpro
  CALL METHOD go_docking->link
    EXPORTING
      repid                        = syst-repid
      dynnr                        = '0100'
*       CONTAINER                  =
    EXCEPTIONS
      OTHERS                       = 4.
  IF sy-subrc <> 0.
*   MESSAGE ID SY-MSGID TYPE SY-MSGTY NUMBER SY-MSGNO
*              WITH SY-MSGV1 SY-MSGV2 SY-MSGV3 SY-
MSGV4.
  ENDIF.
```

However, if you add the name of the container on your screen to the method call, the container will link to this screen element:

```
" Link the docking container to the custom control
element on target dynpro
  CALL METHOD go_docking->link
    EXPORTING
      repid                          = syst-repid
      dynnr                          = '0100'
      CONTAINER                 = '<my container on
screen>'
    EXCEPTIONS
      OTHERS                         = 4.
  IF sy-subrc <> 0.
*    MESSAGE ID SY-MSGID TYPE SY-MSGTY NUMBER SY-MSGNO
*               WITH SY-MSGV1 SY-MSGV2 SY-MSGV3 SY-
MSGV4.
  ENDIF.
```

Question 115: Demo program

What is the code for demo program?

A: See “abapdocu” for more demo program.

Question 116: Scripts

How do we print dollars in scripts instead of rupees?

How do we convert the rupees into dollars?

A: You can use function module DRM_CONVERT_CURRENCY to convert amount from one currency to another.

There will be a Table-Field to print the Dollars symbols. Look at the table so that you will get the field for the Dollar Symbols

If you convert the rupees into dollar, use:
FM CONVERT_TO_FOREIGN_CURRENCY

If you convert the dollar into rupees, then use:
CONVERT_TO_LOCAL_CURRENCY

Question 117: Call transaction

What is the main difference between the SAP scripts and reports?

A: The difference is the script is an integration toll and the report is user defined. Some types of templates can be designed through script, but not possible through reports.

In Reports, you cannot change the font. In Scripts, you can easily change the font size and you can also add logos very easily.

Question 118: Smart forms

What is the main difference between scripts and smartforms?

What are we using in real time, scripts or smart forms?

A: Differences with Smartforms and Sap Scripts:

a) Multiple page formats are possible in smartforms which is not the case in SAPScripts.
b) It is possible to have a smartform without a main window.
c) Labels cannot be created in smartforms.
d) Routines can be written in smartforms tool.
e) Smartforms generates a function module when activated.

The main differences of scripts and smartforms:

Srcipts:
Client dependent
Language dependent
Paragraph mandatory
Main window mandatory

Smartforms:
Client independent
Language independent
Background logos possible

In real time, it depends upon the requirement we are using scripts and smartforms.

Question 119: Dynamic documents format cells

I created a Dynamic Document and inserted a table in it. Now, I want to format some column headers. I want some of them to have 'Left Alignment' and others 'Center Alignment'.

Is it possible to format only the header columns and not the table rows?

The only way that I know to do align format is using the method 'SET_COLUMN_STYLE'. But with this, I format the entire column and that's not what I want.

A: You can try to use the approach in this program: DD_ADD_TABLE

Or you can also just add plain html code which can handle that like the following:

```
<cl_dd_document>->ADD_STATIC_HTML
```

Question 120: Internal and external email

I need to create an email through my program (Module-pool program). On click of a push button, an internal (external) email should be generated.

How can I do it?

A: You can create a button in your module pool program.

```
inside the function code

If function code = <your function code name>../

l_wa_content-line = 'Dear user'.
APPEND l_wa_content TO l_it_content.

l_wa_recieve-receiver = 'NAZ@REDIFF.COM'
l_wa_recieve-rec_type = 'U'. "internet mail
APPEND l_wa_recieve TO l_it_recieve.
clear l_wa_recieve.

l_wa_recieve-receiver = 'PAZZ@REDIFF>COM'
l_wa_recieve-rec_type = 'U'. "internet mail
APPEND l_wa_recieve TO l_it_recieve.
clear l_wa_recieve.

CALL FUNCTION 'SO_NEW_DOCUMENT_SEND_API1'
EXPORTING
document_data = l_wa_document
document_type = 'RAW'
put_in_outbox = 'X'
commit_work = 'X"
TABLES
object_content =
receivers = l_it_recieve
EXCEPTIONS
too_many_receivers = 1
document_not_sent = 2
document_type_not_exist = 3
operation_no_authorization = 4
parameter_error = 5
x_error = 6
enqueue_error = 7
OTHERS = 8.

IF sy-subrc <> 0.
* MESSAGE ID SY-MSGID TYPE SY-MSGTY NUMBER SY-MSGNO
* WITH SY-MSGV1 SY-MSGV2 SY-MSGV3 SY-MSGV4.
ENDIF.
```

```
endif.
```

Later, check the SOST Tcode if your mail is not in the waiting status. If it's not, then the mail is send.

This is the complete code:

```
DATA : l_wa_content TYPE solisti1,
l_wa_recieve TYPE somlreci1.

*Local internal table
DATA : l_it_content TYPE STANDARD TABLE OF solisti1,
l_it_recieve TYPE STANDARD TABLE OF somlreci1.

*in contents you can add the body of the mail

CLEAR l_wa_content.
l_wa_content-line = 'Dear Customer,'.
APPEND l_wa_content TO l_it_content.

CLEAR l_wa_content.
APPEND l_wa_content TO l_it_content. *appending blank
line

CONCATENATE 'TEST' 'MAIL!' 'How r u' INTO l_v_text
SEPARATED BY space.
l_wa_content-line = l_v_text.
APPEND l_wa_content TO l_it_content.


*Reciptents Mail Ids
l_wa_recieve-receiver = 'your mail id'.
l_wa_recieve-rec_type = 'U'. "this is for internet
APPEND l_wa_recieve TO l_it_recieve.
clear l_wa_recieve.

*If you need tyo send to you sap inbox TCODE SBWP
(you can check mail in SBWP), do this:

l_wa_recieve-receiver = 'your user id of SAP'.
l_wa_recieve-rec_type = 'B'. "for SAP user
APPEND l_wa_recieve TO l_it_recieve.
clear l_wa_recieve.

*Heading of the mail
l_wa_document-obj_name = 'TEST MAIL'.
l_wa_document-obj_langu = sy-langu.

*this FM send mail..
CALL FUNCTION 'SO_NEW_DOCUMENT_SEND_API1'
EXPORTING
document_data = l_wa_document
document_type = 'RAW'
```

```
put_in_outbox = c_x
commit_work = c_x
TABLES
object_content = l_it_content
receivers = l_it_recieve
EXCEPTIONS
too_many_receivers = 1
document_not_sent = 2
document_type_not_exist = 3
operation_no_authorization = 4
parameter_error = 5
x_error = 6
enqueue_error = 7
OTHERS = 8.

IF sy-subrc <> 0.
* MESSAGE ID SY-MSGID TYPE SY-MSGTY NUMBER SY-MSGNO
* WITH SY-MSGV1 SY-MSGV2 SY-MSGV3 SY-MSGV4.
ENDIF.
```

Question 121: Functionality of GOS Toolbox for IW22 code-driven or config-driven

Inside a custom piece of code, I have duplicated the "GOS ToolBox" toolbar that SAP displays inside IW22 for attaching documents, pictures, etc. to notifications. The code to pop this toolbox isn't much:

```
CLASS lcl_event_receiver IMPLEMENTATION.
  METHOD on_function_selected.

    DATA:
      ls_lporb              TYPE sibflporb,
      ls_lpor               TYPE sibflpor,
      ls_borident           TYPE boriden


    CASE fcode.
      WHEN '%GOS_TOOLBOX'.
        ls_borident-objkey = viqmel-qmnum.
        ls_borident-objtype = 'BUS2038'.

        CREATE OBJECT go_manager.


        CALL METHOD go_manager->display_toolbox
          EXPORTING
            is_object        = ls_borident
            is_bc_object     = ls_lpor
          EXCEPTIONS
            OTHERS        = 2.

    ENDCASE.

  ENDMETHOD.                          "lcl_my_event_handler
```

But when my toolbox pops, it does not have the same functionality as the GOS toolbox that pops under SAP control in IW22 itself.

In particular, the "create menu" in my toolbox only has "Store Business Document" active. But the "create menu" in the SAP IW22 toolbox has all of the following active:

Create document
Create note
Create external document (URL)

Store business document

So my questions are:
1) Where is SAP IW22 getting its "model" for what's functional in the create menu?

2) Do I need to set up a "customer version" of this "model" to duplicate the SAP functionality?

3) If so, is this a "config" function or is it done somewhere else?

A: The following coding is tested in both a 46c system as well as a NetWeaver 7.0 system. In both cases, I get all options under "Create" except for the last one.

```
REPORT zrich_0001.

data: docking type ref to cl_gui_docking_container.
data: go_manager type ref to cl_gos_manager.

data: ls_borident        type borident.
data: repid type sy-repid.

parameters: p_check.

at selection-screen output.

  repid = sy-repid.
  create object docking
              exporting repid       = repid
                        dynnr       = sy-dynnr
                        side        = docking-
>dock_at_left
                        extension = 1500.

  ls_borident-objkey = '000010000001'.
  ls_borident-objtype = 'BUS2038'.

  create object go_manager.
  call method go_manager->display_toolbox
    exporting
      io_container     = docking
      is_object        = ls_borident
    exceptions
      others        = 2.
```

Check if you need to implement BADI "GOS_SRV_REQUEST" to get accesibility to the methods of CL_BDS_DOCUMENT_SET.

The reason for this is that the customer wants to maintain

picture attachments in IW22 via the standard SAP toolbox invoked from the title bar, but wants me to display the first three attached pictures in the fifth custom subscreen of an IW22 custom tab.

You should use the 'get_info' method of CL_BDS_DOCUMENT_SET to find out what's there, and then figure out how to retrieve the pictures and pop them into picture controls.

In your global definitions, you can use the following:

```
data: GO_MANAGER Type Ref To CL_GOS_VIEW_MANAGER.
```

Instead, use its subclass:

```
data: GO_MANAGER Type Ref To CL_GOS_MANAGER.
```

You should then see all of the options (except the last one) in your toolbox.

Question 122: Container refresh

I am working on an interactive OOALV, where I am using the 'handle_double_click' event to get the details of a particular cell. When I go back to the original screen and double click a different cell, in debugging mode I was able to get the correct values. But on the output, it is only showing the previous value.

I am using the method 'set_table_for_first_display' only to display the values.

What should I do?

A: Check if you are changing the values of the table you are passing to the second screen. My suggestion would be to use the method 'set_table' only once. After that, just use the method 'refresh_table_display'.

Another suggestion is in the PBO module, include this as the last statement:

```
call method grid->refresh_table_display.
```

In PAI module, include this as the FIRST statement:

```
call method grid->check_changed_data.
```

You can also try to do this in PBO as follows:

```
IF custom_container IS INITIAL.

CREATE OBJECT custom_container
EXPORTING
container_name = cont_on_100.

CREATE OBJECT grid
EXPORTING i_parent = custom_container.

CALL METHOD grid1->set_table_for_first_display
EXPORTING is_layout = gs_layout
CHANGING it_fieldcatalog = it_fieldcat
it_outtab = ti_arquivo[]
it_sort = isort1[].

ELSE.
CALL METHOD grid->refresh_table_display.
```

```
ENDIF.
```

Another way is to call the method 'refresh_table_display' to refresh the values which are displayed on the grid:

syantax:

```
CALL METHOD grid->refresh_table_display.
```

In the above statement, <grid> is the instance of the class CL_GUI_ALV_GRID.

It has no mandatory parameters. Now, you call the event handler method for getting the exact cell values.

Question 123: Returning values

How can I get the value from a returning parameter when we call a method from the main program?

```
call method obj1->withdraw exporting amount = 100
NEW_BALANCE = obj1->deposit.
```

New balance is my returning parameter of the method, but at the same time I have to export some values too to that method.

It's not working for me.

A: Check first if this method has return parameters.

There are a few ways, but this one is commonly preferred 'SOME_VALUE'. It's the returning parameter.

```
data: some_value type i.

some_value = obj1->get_some_value( ).
```

You can still use this syntax. Here, the IM_VALUE is your importing parameter.

```
NEW_BALANCE = obj1->deposit ( im_value = 100).
```

In addition to the code:

```
new_balance = obj1->deposit('some value').
```

You can use the following syntax also:

```
CALL METHOD obj1->deposit
  EXPORTING
    iv_value   = 'some value'
  RECEIVING
    iv_balance = new_balance.
```

You can use the other form also:

```
<data> = obj1->withdraw ( exporting amount = 100 ).
```

or:

```
call method obj1->withdraw
exporting amount = 100
receiving <parameter> = <data>.
```

Question 124: Reverse Method

```
CALL METHOD obj1->deposit
EXPORTING
iv_value = 'some value'
RECEIVING
iv_balance (main program parameter) =
new_balance(returning parameter).
```

When I use this one, it stated that the reverse is accepted and it's throwing a syntax error.

E.g.

```
CALL METHOD obj1->deposit
EXPORTING
iv_value = 'some value'
RECEIVING
new_balance(returning parameter) = iv_balance (main
program parameter).
```

The output is coming as zero, as the program parameter value is Zero.

A: If the returning parameter is defined as NEW_BALANCE within the method, then the following should work fine. But you must move some result to this parameter inside the method itself.

```
CALL METHOD obj1->deposit
EXPORTING
iv_value = 'some value'
RECEIVING
new_balance = iv_balance .
```

So for example, you should be filling it inside this method: method deposit.

```
  new_balance = 100.  "or whatever your logic is

endmethod.
```

Also check if you're missing on that part where some operation has to be carried out for the parameter which you're returning.

Question 125: Macro

What is MACRO in ABAP?

How does it work?

A: DEFINE macro.

Effect

Defines a section of source code (macro) that you can address using the name macro. Source code saved as a DEFINE macro may only consist of complete ABAP statements.

All macro used are expanded fully in translation. Macros are a text substitute for the translation phase, not a modularization technique for runtime use.

You conclude a macro with the 'END-OF-DEFINITION' statement.

When you define a macro, you can use placeholders (&n, where n = 1, 2, ..., 9). When the macro is expanded, '&n' is replaced with the 'n-th' current parameter.

Example:
Suppose you define a macro "INCREMENT" which you then use in your program:

```
DEFINE INCREMENT.
ADD 1 TO &1.
END-OF-DEFINITION.

DATA: NUMBER TYPE I VALUE 1.
...
INCREMENT NUMBER.
```

Notes:
As a rule, you should use subroutines (FORM, FUNCTION) instead of macros. This is because subroutines unlike macros, are supported by all of the ABAP Workbench tools (debugging, runtime analysis, runtime error handling, etc.).

You cannot define a macro within a macro using the DEFINE statement.

You cannot use an ABAP keyword as a macro name.

The validity of a macro definition is determined by its position in the source code. You can use a given macro in any line of code following its definition. There is no distinction between global and local macros. For example, the fact that a macro is defined within a subroutine has no effect on its validity.

If you redefine a macro, that is, assign a new meaning to an existing name, the new meaning takes effect from the position in the program where the macro was redefined.

Here's a simple piece of code:

```
DEFINE col_name.
read table it_fldcat into wa_it_fldcat index &1.
wa_it_fldcat-coltext = &2.
modify it_fldcat from wa_it_fldcat index &1.

end-of-definition.


Now in my main program:

****** code
ASSIGN wa_elements TO <fs1>.

CREATE OBJECT z_object EXPORTING z_object = z_object.
* i_parent = grid_container1.
CALL METHOD z_object->build_dynamic_structures
CHANGING it_fldcat = it_fldcat.
*
```

* Dynamic field cat is returned with dynamic table

* Here before displaying the table, you can change the field * catalog to adjust your own names.
* The above Method call just uses the
* names in the table structure.

```
col_name 1 'Customer'.
col_name 2 'Name'.
col_name 3 'Street'.
col_name 4 'Phone'.
col_name 5 'City'.
col_name 6 'Post Code'.
```

Without using the macro, I'd have to write loads more code such as:

```
read table it_fldcat into wa_it_fldcat index 1.
wa_it_fldcat-coltext = 'Customer
modify it_fldcat from wa_it_fldcat index 1.

read table it_fldcat into wa_it_fldcat index 2.
wa_it_fldcat-coltext = 'Name'
modify it_fldcat from wa_it_fldcat index2 .
```

and so on.

You can see here that a function call or a subroutine call is OF NO USE IN THIS INSTANCE, nor is this code any use as an INCLUDE since it's only applicable to the case used in this program.

The macro is being used simply as a shorthand way of generating a lot of repetitive code quickly and simply.

With more variables, it becomes even more useful. But the downside is that if you have an error in the macro, then it's sometimes very hard to find as you don't step through each line like in normall debugging.

Index

CPSIA information can be obtained
at www.ICGtesting.com
Printed in the USA
BVOW03s2056101216
470440BV00007B/108/P